RESILIENT GARDEN

RESILIENT GARDEN

SUSTAINABLE GARDENING FOR A CHANGING CLIMATE

TOM MASSEY

CHAPTER 4
CLIMATE RESILIENT GARDEN DESIGN
092

CHAPTER 5
RESILIENT PLANT GUIDE
156

CHAPTER 6
SUSTAINABLE MATERIALS
206

WWW.DK.COM/RESILIENT-GARDEN

CHAPTER ONE

RESPONDING TO CLIMATE CHANGE

[Above] My mother gave me a small area of our garden to experiment with when I was a child, and my fascination with gardening rapidly developed.
[Left] Thirty years later, I am pictured in my garden for Yeo Valley Organic at the RHS Chelsea Flower Show 2021.

THE MAKING OF A GARDEN DESIGNER

A question I am often asked is, "What inspired you to become a garden designer?" It's a hard question to answer succinctly, because the answer is so multifaceted; there are many factors that influenced my decision to pursue this career.

Starting at the beginning, I grew up in Richmond upon Thames, a leafy suburb in southwest London. We had a small back garden, typical of a London terraced house, and my mother—a keen gardener—gave me an area to call my own. I was allowed to experiment, choosing a variety of plants on exciting trips to the garden center to try out in combination. I remember being fascinated by the huge array of color, form, texture, habit, scent, and all the other attributes plants could display. I was moved by the change of the seasons, seeing green shoots emerge; followed by flowers, fruit, and berries; then bare winter stems. The plants changed the look, atmosphere, and character of the space and they could even affect my mood. At the time I didn't know it, but on looking back I can see this was an early foray into the world of garden design, with my successes and failures acting as an important learning experience.

We also had a small allotment, and understanding that we could grow plants to eat was a revelation. My mother was a fervent believer in the importance of good-quality organic food. We always had fresh organic fruit and vegetables in the house, some home-grown, some store-bought. Seeing produce grow and ripen, to be harvested when ready to eat, gave me a newfound respect for plants. I learned that they could provide for us, nourishing both the body and the soul.

> I felt elation when successes were achieved: seeing a flower open and develop into a fruit, then plucking and eating that fruit, savoring the succulent and sweet flesh.

When plants died, I felt devastated. How could I have failed the plant? How could I have let it die? On the flip side of the coin, I felt elation when successes were achieved: seeing a flower open and develop into a fruit, then plucking and eating that fruit, savoring the succulent and sweet flesh. I felt an overwhelming sense of achievement that this was something that had been produced by my hard work and patience.

Looking back, gardening and growing plants was a formative experience, and my successes and failures were important in learning about both the frailties and the resilience of life. It was a process in which I could escape the mundanity of daily existence, and it was the start of a deep love of and connection to the natural world. I am eternally grateful for that introduction at a young age.

009

FORMATIVE LANDSCAPES

My two younger brothers and I were regularly forced to undertake long walks. Every day, come rain or shine, whether we wanted to or not, we were marched up to Richmond Park and encouraged to run wild. This was a ploy to get us to expend some energy, three lively small boys being a bit of a handful—but that early connection to a landscape forged a deep and profound love of it that persists to this day.

Richmond Park is an amazing place, a site of both national and international importance for wildlife conservation. It has been designated as a Site of Special Scientific Interest (SSSI), a National Nature Reserve (NNR), and a Special Area of Conservation (SAC). The park is full of veteran oaks that are hundreds of years old, rich with complex detail, character, and incredible ecosystems. They also make dynamic climbing frames!

Invertebrate life is particularly abundant: billions of yellow meadow ants have sculpted the landscape of acidic grassland, and their relationship with the green woodpeckers that feed on them is of particular scientific interest. As a child jumping from mound to mound, I had no idea about the complex ecosystems and interconnected life forms coexisting beneath my feet in the soil, as well as on the trees and in the air. From the micro (ants and insects) to the macro (trees, birds, and the wild deer that roam the park), that early connection to nature led me to want to study, observe, and interact with it in deeper and more meaningful ways as I grew older.

[Above] A scene typical of Richmond Park, which contains an estimated 1,300 veteran oak trees, of which 320 are classed as ancient.
[Left] There are an estimated 3 billion yellow meadow ants residing in the richly biodiverse landscape of Richmond Park. Together, they weigh about the same as 125 of their fellow residents, the fallow deer. Some of the 400,000 anthills have been found to be more than 150 years old.

[Above] In Cornwall, the coastal cliff face has always fascinated me. How can plants grow out of a sheer rock face, battered by wild salt and spray, frozen in winter and scorched in summer, surviving rock falls and landslides, recolonizing quickly after devastating events? There is so much to be inspired by and so much to learn from.

[Right] Coastal plants can thrive in extremely harsh environments. Here, *Carpobrotus edulis* (pigface) and *Crithmum maritimum* (rock samphire) are growing out of an almost vertical rock face on the Lizard Peninsula, the southernmost point in Cornwall.

Another landscape that exerted a profound effect on me was the rugged beauty of the Roseland Peninsula in Cornwall. Every summer, my family would decamp to a tiny hamlet near Portscatho on the south coast. The azure waters, gnarled coastal woodlands, wildflower-filled pastures, and rocky coastal landscapes provided an amazing adventure ground. My grandparents had a friend in the hamlet, wonderfully named Dick Twist, who owned a beautiful, crumbling, and ancient house where we used to stay. He would spend the summer holidays studying Stonehenge, and we would occupy his house with cousins and family friends. The house was cold and damp, filled with mice, voles, spiders, and other insects. The beds were stiff and hard and it definitely wasn't comfortable, but it had an incredible atmosphere. A hushed and reverent magic emanated from the fabric of the building, and the garden in particular was a place of wonder and excitement.

I can still vividly remember the scent of lavender on a hot summer day, and getting lost among wildflowers and weeds that hummed with grasshoppers and bees. The garden was full of forgotten wonders; greenhouses that were covered in climbers, filled with triffidlike tomato plants, filling the air inside with their pungent perfume; summerhouses with stunning sea views hidden behind overgrown hedges; apple orchards lost to seas of savage stinging nettles. The garden was gradually being reclaimed by nature, slowly being lost to the wild, while still retaining an imprint and memory of its man-made self.

It was a magical thing to witness, this yearly degradation of a garden into an increasingly natural space as the rugged Cornish landscape, fervent and fertile, slowly reclaimed it. My connection with this space was, and still is, profound. It lives on vividly in memories, and I still return there in dreams. But, as with most beautiful and fragile things, it came to an end. Dick died, and the house was sold. Both the house and garden were sterilized, modernized, and relandscaped, Cornish nature banished to the boundaries. Worse still, it sat empty for years, with the only signs of life being regular gardening to keep out the wild; manicured lawns, pristine paving, and clipped hedges were all perfectly maintained.

This made a deep impression on me and forced me to question what constitutes a garden. How is it different from a landscape? Can the two coexist, and could we not work with nature to achieve a more profound and harmonious result? I was a teenager when I first formed these thoughts, and although at that point I had other ambitions—I was keen on drawing and went on to do a BA honors degree in animation—they returned to me constantly, and still do. How can we embrace the wild force of nature and not fight it? How can we be inspired by it, utilize it, and engage with it to create successful, harmonious, and magical spaces? Landscape or garden—do we need a distinction?

RADICAL GARDENS

RADICAL AND RESILIENT GARDEN DESIGN HAS BEEN EMPLOYED THROUGHOUT HISTORY AND IN EXTREME SITUATIONS TO PURSUE SURVIVAL AND PROVIDE HOPE. WE NEED TO LEARN FROM THE INSPIRING PIONEERS OF THESE GARDENS SO THAT WE CAN BECOME THE RADICALS OF THE FUTURE.

I have always been excited and inspired by all things radical. My first show garden at RHS Hampton Court Palace Flower Show in 2016 was inspired by the resilience of refugees. Entitled "Border Control," it was sponsored by the UN Refugee Agency (UNHCR) and designed in collaboration with a friend, John Ward. The garden used British native and non-native plants as a metaphor to represent British residents and refugees. A central, seemingly British wildflower meadow thrived on an island surrounded by a wide moat and a razor-wire fence, while non-native plants struggled to survive in rubble and desolation outside. Amid the rubble, some plants bloomed: colorful jewels of hope and resilience in the harsh environment, small displays of strength in the face of adversity.

To enter the central meadow, visitors first had to pass through a turnstile and show a border guard a pass, adding to the theatrical experience. Once inside, the British meadow could be viewed in closer proximity. Woven among the British native plants was an array of non-native species from the outer rubble zone. These plants had made

Woven among the British native plants was an array of non-native species from the outer rubble zone. These plants had made the leap and were adding to the beauty, biodiversity, and harmony of the planting; they were a simple metaphor for the benefits of inclusion.

the leap and were adding to the beauty, biodiversity, and harmony of the planting; they were a simple metaphor for the benefits of inclusion and integration. I remember many of the conversations that arose at the show. So many people were moved, some to tears—including the RHS judges—by the stories woven into the garden.

Strewn amid the rubble were toys, life jackets, and items of clothing that had washed up on Greek beaches—lost possessions from people making a perilous journey. A journey which, for many, would have been their last. Other visitors questioned, "How could this be called a 'garden?'" I remember the almost incandescent rage that emanated from some people: "There is rubble and waste! It's not beautiful!"

01

02

03

[01] This view of the "Border Control" garden from beyond the razor-wire fence and heavy-duty turnstile gives visitors a sense of how it feels to be unwelcome. [02] *Salvia nemorosa* 'Ostfriesland' thriving in the rubble just outside the razor-wire fence. [03] A bright poppy growing out of the rubble: a glimmer of hope representing resilience and determination emerging from destruction.

Even then, in my early career, I was questioning whether a garden needs to be beautiful. What is beauty? Is it only the traditional postcard-picture version of it that should be applauded and revered? Is there not also beauty in resilience, decay, and destruction?

THE LEMON TREE TRUST

This show garden led to me being introduced to the Lemon Tree Trust, with a view to designing a show garden at the RHS Chelsea Flower Show to promote its work. This is a charity that engages with refugees, encouraging gardening in harsh camp environments. One of the most profound and inspiring trips of my life was a visit to Domiz 1, a refugee camp where staff from the Trust were working, near the Syrian border in Northern Kurdish Iraq. The research trip was an opportunity to speak to people in the camp, one gardener to another. I wanted to understand why they were gardening and what benefits it brought them while they lived in the difficult situation of forced migration and displacement. I had some incredible conversations and heard stories of people who had the presence of mind to take a cutting of a favorite rose, or a selection of seeds, before fleeing for their lives. These plants were so important that they could not be left behind. But what was it that the gardens brought to the harsh, dry, and dusty camp environment, where water, such a precious resource, was so scarce? It was a sense of home, a small reminder of better times, a glimmer of hope, and a sense of order; the very process of sowing, growing, and gardening restored some normality to broken and devastated lives.

[01] Even in limited space, and with scarce resources, ornamentals and edibles can be grown together. [02] The Azadi Community garden in Domiz 1 camp in Northern Kurdish Iraq is a green space within the camp for gardeners to come together and build a sense of community. It provides some respite from the harsh environment.

02

04

[03] The Trust pilots agricultural businesses and gardening initiatives in refugee communities, creating employment opportunities and restoring cultural identity, dignity, and purpose.
[04] Resilient plants are common in the camp, like this drought-tolerant *Gazania*. The dry, dusty environment requires creative and resilient planting solutions.

I was awed by the way these people were using landscaping and garden design for human benefit, creating shade from the searing heat by growing tough, drought-tolerant, and fast-growing trees and plants; producing food where food was scarce; and designing hushed, sheltered, and calm courtyards to escape to. These gardens were wide-ranging and beautiful. The plants were growing in almost impossibly difficult conditions, but the gardeners were skillfully using all the resources available to them: waste materials were turned into shelters, structures, and planters; gray water was diverted and collected in containers; rills and channels were used for irrigation. The gardeners learned from friends and neighbors, sharing knowledge and skills across the community. It was a profound learning experience for me. This truly was radical gardening, designing for the environment in which these people were forced to live. They were resilient gardeners by necessity. This forced change was unwelcome and unavoidable, enacted by powers outside of their control. What was so inspiring was their willingness, ingenuity, and determination to adapt, to survive, and to thrive.

Yet we are all going to have to become more radical and flexible as the planet we live on is threatened. Dramatic and rapid changes to the world we live in are happening before our eyes. Global powers have been criticized for sleepwalking into an emergency, and now the changes that were predicted by scientists and science fiction writers are here: warming climates, increasingly unpredictable weather, droughts, floods, and rising sea levels.

Fortunately, human beings have been capable of adapting since the dawn of time. It is our modus operandi. Our large brains are an evolutionary advantage that make us ingenious. Now is the time for ingenuity, experimentation, grit, and determination. We should look to teachings of the past for inspiration, to the radicals of previous eras who dared to try something different. We should also pay heed to the radicals of the present, the pioneers flouting the rigid teachings of textbooks that will soon be outdated as the rules have to change. We need to become the radicals of the future. We are the pioneer gardeners, growers, designers, architects, engineers, botanists, farmers, horticulturists, planners, and global leaders who can and must adapt. Our very existence is threatened. Just like the inspiring people living in the Domiz camp, we have no choice.

[Above] Drought-resilient Mediterranean-inspired planting in the Lemon Tree Trust Garden at Chelsea Flower Show in 2018; the planting scheme, tough and hardy but also colorful and uplifting, was inspired by the gardens of Domiz 1 camp and what people there were growing.
[Left] I used a palette of resilient and drought-tolerant planting for the Lemon Tree Trust Garden at Chelsea Flower Show, inspired by what I saw in the Domiz 1 Camp gardens.

[Top] In the Ruin Garden by Tanja Lincke, a dilapidated building has been transformed into a real ruin, artfully capturing the romantic atmosphere of a disused industrial site.
[Right] The rawness of the hard material is contrasted with seemingly wild planting, characterized by loose perennials; grasses; and trees such as birch, pine, and staghorn sumac (*Rhus typhina*).

RESILIENT LANDSCAPES

THE POWER OF NATURE TO SURVIVE IN CHALLENGING CONDITIONS IS TRULY INSPIRING, WHETHER YOU SEE A SINGLE PLANT EMERGING FROM A CRACK IN A CONCRETE PAVEMENT OR A CONTAMINATED BROWNFIELD SITE FULL OF BIODIVERSITY. NATURE WILL ADAPT TO CLIMATE CHANGE—BUT THE BIG QUESTION IS, HOW WILL WE?

Harsh landscapes define resilience and offer us lessons that are far more profound than the quick fix offered by chemical fertilizers, pesticides, and watering-intensive maintenance regimes. Resources worldwide will become scarcer as populations increase and the climate changes. We need to learn to be less wasteful. Being inspired by nature and by resilient landscapes is key to the success of resilient garden design, as we plan for the changing climate. By looking at nature and how it deals with extreme conditions or events, we can find the answers we need.

This thinking can be applied to general landscape and garden design. There are so many books, resources, talks, and lectures on the subject that sometimes the information can be overwhelming. Learning from the past is important, of course, but so is experimentation. If everyone always followed the rules, did as others have done before them, then nothing would ever progress. It is the radicals, the innovators, the forward-thinking practitioners and designers willing to try something new who may enact meaningful change. Often, these people have been inspired by radical landscapes or experiences that set their world alight, sparked an interest, or triggered an idea. Climate change is one such experience to which we are all going to have to adapt.

CHAPTER TWO

WHAT IS RESILIENT GARDENING?

A CALL TO ACTION

WE ARE IN THE MIDST OF A CLIMATE EMERGENCY, FACING THE REALITY OF A SUBSTANTIAL LOSS OF BIODIVERSITY, WITH THREATS TO OUR LOCAL FLORA AND FAUNA BY INVASIVE SPECIES AND A STEADILY WARMING PLANET.

This is on top of mounting societal crises as we see ever-rising levels of mental, physical, and social health issues, all of which were magnified by the COVID-19 pandemic. However, while world events can seem to be daunting and relentless, leaving us feeling impotent, our gardens and outdoor spaces are places where we can enact visible change. They also offer us a respite from the pressures of daily life; tending to them gives us something meaningful to focus on.

HUMAN EFFECTS

As custodians of this planet—the dominant sentient beings—we have to acknowledge that our own actions have caused the crises that loom. We have sleepwalked into a series of environmental disasters that are slowly unfolding before our eyes. Over the past few years, I am sure we can all think of ways in which we have experienced the effects firsthand: more extreme weather; yearly temperature records eclipsed; plastic pollution everywhere, from the remotest beaches to the highest mountains; loss of habitat due to urbanization; and free-falling biodiversity decline.

This translates to our garden spaces, too, where you may have observed flowers blooming weeks earlier than usual. Higher rainfall and extreme weather events lead to flooding; swamped plants; and winds that can bring down trees, blow away sheds, or tear down walls. You may have also experienced drought and relied heavily on irrigation to keep your plants from dying. Wildlife is disappearing from our gardens, too. With the overuse of harmful chemicals, too much hard landscaping, and artificial plants and lawns, it is no wonder that these spaces can be hostile, offering wildlife no natural habitat.

01

[01] Workers in the Philippines sorting through mountains of plastic waste. [02] Flooded houses in the Windsor suburb near Sydney, Australia, where the Hawkesbury River burst its banks due to torrential rain in 2022. [03] Wildfires in Australia: in 2020, more than 24 million acres (10 million hectares) were burnt. People's lives and homes and an estimated 3 billion wild animals were detrimentally affected.

02

03

"DELAY IN CONCERTED
GLOBAL ACTION WILL MISS
A BRIEF AND RAPIDLY
CLOSING WINDOW TO SECURE
A LIVABLE FUTURE."

PROFESSOR HANS-OTTO PÖRTNER,
IPCC WORKING GROUP II CO-CHAIR

In February 2022, the Royal Society in London published a report that looked at the first flowering times of plants, using more than 400,000 studies and starting as far back as 1753. It found that flowering timings varied year on year based on fluctuating temperatures, but ultimately, a 2.2°F (1.2°C) temperature rise has advanced flowering times, and therefore spring, by a full month. Between 1987 and 2019, plants in the UK were flowering a month earlier than they did before this period.

But a rapidly changing climate means early-blooming flowers are not the only indication of a dramatic shift in the natural order of things. There have been earlier sightings of migrating wildlife, birds nesting ahead of schedule, and insects premature to the party before flowers have emerged. All of these shifting timetables could become even more wildly out of sync if we stay on our current course, throwing the delicate ecosystem into dysfunction and having drastic cumulative effects. For example, pollinators may emerge to find that the blooms they rely on have come and gone. This could then affect bird populations that rely on those insects for food.

Ulf Büntgen, lead author of the Royal Society report and professor of environmental systems analysis at the University of Cambridge, warns that "ecological mismatch" could have a damaging impact. "If the trends continue like this, that could have more profound effects, severe effects, on the functioning and productivity of ecosystems, because things that depend on each other in terms of timing—insects, plants, other animals—get disrupted."

How can we gardeners help? The answer is to grow a range of adaptable plants that cover a long period of flowering, extending the season during which food is available to pollinating insects.

SOLASTALGIA

Solastalgia is a word coined by Glenn Albrecht, an environmental philosopher and an honorary associate in the School of Geosciences, the University of Sydney, New South Wales, Australia. It first appeared in print in an essay written by Albrecht entitled "Solastalgia: A New Concept in Human Health and Identity," published in 2005. Using the concept of "nostalgia" as a starting point, solastalgia is an amalgamation of the Latin word *sōlācium*, meaning comfort, or solace, and the suffix *-algia*, from Greek, indicating pain in specified parts of the body. It describes the solace of home and the pain of its loss: it is the feeling when one's sense of place and belonging are threatened by climate change. In other words, it is homesickness while you are still home, and distress at your home being destroyed while you are still living there.

SHIFTING SEASONS

DUE TO RISING TEMPERATURES, SPRING FLOWERS ARE BLOOMING A MONTH EARLIER IN THE UK. THIS IS NOT THE ONLY INDICATION THAT OUR DELICATE ECOSYSTEM IS BEING THROWN OUT OF BALANCE, WHICH MAY LEAD TO CATASTROPHIC CONSEQUENCES.

This apple tree blossomed early before being hit with low temperatures and snow, which caused the plant damage from the cold and limited its harvest.

MAKING A DIFFERENCE

A LACK OF COMMITMENT FROM GOVERNMENTS AND A SLOW-TO-ACT ETHOS CAN MAKE THE FUTURE LOOK DAUNTING, BUT THERE ARE MANY THINGS THAT WE, AS GARDENERS, CAN CONTRIBUTE. WE CAN CHANNEL OUR ANXIETY INTO ACTION; NEGATIVE EMOTIONS CAN BE THE DRIVERS OF CHANGE.

We have probably all questioned what difference our individual actions could make in the face of such a monumental threat—but if we all commit to making small changes, it can lead to a huge net effect. A simple example from an RHS study is that if every UK gardener planted a medium-sized tree—such as a cherry tree, crabapple tree, or birch—in their community, school, workplace, or garden and nurtured it to maturity, these trees would store carbon the equivalent of driving 11.4 million times around the planet. Trees have so many positive effects, from supporting wildlife with habitats and food sources to human benefits such as providing shade, cooling hot summer temperatures, increasing well-being, and removing pollutants from the air we breathe. Even dead trees are beneficial to the environment, as degrading wood provides habitats and food sources for many species of insects, plants, fungi, and animals.

CONNECTING WITH NATURE

When we as a society feel more connected to nature and the world around us, our desire to protect it is cultivated. With a growing urban population, and pandemics a real threat, the presence of gardens and attractive green public spaces as places for respite is increasingly vital for our health and well-being. Despite all the portents of disaster, and the destruction of the planet's fragile ecosystems that have already occurred, we are living in a time of opportunity for radical change. Landscape design professionals and gardeners have suddenly risen in stock; planners, architects, developers, government ministers, and the heads of corporate businesses realize that a deeper connection to the natural world is not just increasingly desirable but vital and can lead to increased productivity, well-being, and prosperity for society.

[Top] Here, I used *Betula utilis* var. *jacquemontii* in the foreground and a multistemmed *Amelanchier lamarckii* in the background to evoke the feel of a woodland edge.

[Right] Our gardens and green spaces provide us with an essential connection to nature. This garden, which I designed for a client, provides an immersive view to draw the inhabitants outside.

GARDENS IN THE LANDSCAPE

We must all reconsider our perspective on what our gardens should look like and how they function. We need to move away from gardens that are designed only to provide aesthetic perfection and instead see our personal outside space as part of a vast landscape. Although individual gardens may be small, they are often adjacent to others, which makes them a valuable environmental resource. We, as custodians of these spaces, can enact change to benefit not only us individually, but also the wider environment and society in general.

We can start to plan now for the changes that we will need to introduce to our gardens. We must design spaces that have the ability to thrive in present conditions and to recover from adverse events predicted for the future: that is the definition of a resilient landscape.

Technological advancements mean that climate scientists can map out our future weather, modeling with increasing accuracy what the local conditions will be like in 5, 10, and even 50 years' time. That means that we can start to plan now for the changes that we will need to introduce to our gardens. We must design spaces that have the ability to thrive in present conditions and to recover from adverse events predicted for the future: that is the definition of a resilient landscape. Rather than seeing the climate emergency as catastrophic for our gardens, we can embrace the opportunities that a changing climate provides.

Through resilient design and the avoidance of products and materials that are unsustainable, reduce biodiversity, or have a high carbon footprint, gardeners and the horticultural industry can help. There are more than 30 million people involved in gardening in the UK alone, and we all have the potential to grow beneficial plants at our homes or in allotments and community spaces.

THE FOOTPRINT OF GARDENS

The total area of gardens in the UK is estimated at approximately 1,670 square miles (433,000 hectares). That's slightly more than a fifth the size of Wales, or approximately the same size as the Cape Verde Islands.

As can be seen here, gardens are not isolated landscapes. They connect to form larger landscapes and green corridors. It is important to allow wildlife to move though and between our gardens to protect local wildlife and promote biodiversity.

01

[01] The "Garden of Eden," a community garden in Manhattan constructed over five years by Adam Purple. In 1973, a building behind Purple's home on Eldridge Street was flattened. He decided to start a garden in the resulting space with his companion, Eve. [02] The resulting garden was 15,000 sq ft (1,494 sq m), featuring 45 trees, including eight black walnuts, and a wide range of produce, including corn, cherry tomatoes, asparagus, and raspberries. He regularly biked to Central Park to collect horse manure to use as fertilizer, and volunteers helped with upkeep. [03] Purple was an activist and urban Edenist and became famous in New York for taking "guerrilla gardening" to new extremes.

03

02

GUIDING PRINCIPLES

**WORKING TOGETHER, SHARING KNOWLEDGE, AND EMBRACING
SUSTAINABLE PRACTICES ARE MEANINGFUL ACTIONS WE CAN TAKE—
IMPERATIVE CONTRIBUTIONS TO THE RESCUE MISSION FOR OUR PLANET.**

In the push to mitigate climate change, let's come together; share ideas; be honest about the challenges; and disseminate knowledge and insights from inspiring books, talks, or events we have attended. Let's encourage a community, connecting with other gardeners either over the fence or across the world on social media. Gardeners need to talk to those in areas with a warmer climate to study what grows well there and adjust their ideas about a garden that will flourish in the long term.

We can combine all our efforts to make a meaningful contribution, providing joined-up, global thinking. We need to be radical, resilient, and willing to change. For this is what humans have always done—we adapt, we survive, we overcome problems by designing solutions to them. We are at a critical point in human history, as the actions we take today will determine the outlook for the planet we inhabit. It's not too late—we gardeners can do our bit, no matter how small it seems, to help save the planet. Let's embrace sustainable and resilient gardens designed for the present day, as well as for the uncertain future. If we can come together as a global gardening community, we are capable of enacting big change. We can edge one step closer to securing the outlook for future gardeners, for the health of our planet, and for the life of future generations.

DESIGN FOR THE ENVIRONMENT

Gardens can be positive for human health: they provide aesthetic beauty, increase well-being, reduce the impact of climatic conditions such as heat and wind, and can reduce the effects of pollution. But gardens can also support wildlife; increase biodiversity; and be naturally resilient to the effects of climate change, drought, flooding, and wind. Creative thinking can produce both aesthetically beautiful and environmentally sustainable gardens.

REDUCE RESOURCES

You can design your garden to need less water, and to avoid reliance upon the use of chemical pesticides and synthetic fertilizers. Circular thinking, zero-waste strategies, rainwater harvesting, and resilience can be built in at the outset.

SOURCE SUSTAINABLE MATERIALS

From responsibly sourced and sustainably produced timber to ethically sourced stone, peat-free compost, and biodegradable pots, be mindful of all the materials and resources you use. Research where your proposed materials come from and question suppliers about production. Make decisions driven not only by aesthetics, durability, and function, but also by sustainability. Can it be maintained long-term? If not, are there sustainable alternatives?

CONSIDER THE SUSTAINABILITY OF THE CONSTRUCTION

Are there products or practices that could reduce the need for concrete? Does a tree really need to be felled? Can you work with the site as it is rather than removing everything and starting from scratch? How can the carbon footprint be reduced? Can waste be recycled or repurposed? If there are better methods that can be used, assess and implement them.

DESIGN WITH TIME IN MIND

The desire for instant gratification—for gardens that "look good all year round"—needs to be abandoned, along with plastic grass and fake plants. Replace harmful chemical pesticides, herbicides, and fertilizers with the growing range of organic and eco-friendly alternatives. A garden is a living, fragile ecosystem, encompassing a complex web of interlinked species and processes. We need to respect nature and understand the web of life so that we coexist with it instead of trying to master it.

INTRODUCE RESILIENT DESIGN

Consider the site and its conditions in the past and present so you can determine the characteristics of the site and work with them, not against them. Be mindful of previous land usage, potential contamination, and average rainfall, as well as present conditions such as soil geology and exposure to the elements—wind, rain, and sun; and today's gardeners must also design for future conditions, climatic changes, and unpredictable weather events.

[Above] This show garden by Sam Ovens at RHS Tatton Park Flower Show celebrated light-touch landscaping: open timber structures floated over a dense matrix of plants.

[Right] On the Yeo Valley Organic show garden, I designed the planting scheme to show that seasonality can be beautiful. The garden was at the first-ever Autumn Chelsea Flower Show (postponed from May due to COVID-19 lockdowns in 2021), so I chose late-season color and plants "going over" to celebrate the colors of the time of year and the ephemeral beauty of flowers in bloom.

GARDENING FOR EVERYONE

TAYSHAN HAYDEN-SMITH is a social activist, guerrilla gardener, and RHS ambassador. He founded Grow2know in 2019 with the aim of making horticulture accessible to all.

Tayshan in Hope Gardens, previously named the Grenfell Garden of Peace. Created with no plan, the garden provided a place for the community to gather and unify in what was a barren space.

WHY DO YOU THINK COMMUNITY GARDENS ARE SO IMPORTANT?

"

Community gardens are where the seeds of change will be sown—a space where people and plants coexist to create social and environmental impact.

I grew up in the shadow of Grenfell Tower in North Kensington, London, where the 2017 fire took 72 lives and left a legacy of trauma, anger, and shock. The response to the tragedy demonstrated the importance of community; with no particular plan, people turned to nature, reclaiming a barren and unloved space. A transformation occurred as the community came together to dig, plant, and talk, and the space became known as the Grenfell Garden of Peace. It was a symbol of hope to many, as community members would walk past to share a smile, a conversation, or to offer their time—often, five minutes would turn into ten, which would turn into an hour, which would turn into days.

THIS EXPERIENCE WAS THE BIRTH OF GROW2KNOW, A GRASS-ROOTS NONPROFIT ORGANIZATION THAT YOU FOUNDED IN 2019. WHAT ARE THE MAIN AIMS OF GROW2KNOW?

The heart of the organization lies in reclaiming space and reconnecting people with nature and each other. Putting community at the forefront in the creation of public, outdoor spaces, we focus on consultation, collaboration, and place-making. We are committed to inspiring a culture change to implement more sustainable systems that promote biodiversity, circular economies, and regenerative practices. We are on a mission to inspire, heal, and educate through horticulture.

HOW IMPORTANT DO YOU THINK IT IS THAT WE MAKE HORTICULTURE ACCESSIBLE TO ALL?

Gardening should be a core skill, as it is through plants that we will start to understand how we can solve both environmental and societal issues. Without education, understanding, or points of access, we are becoming further disconnected from nature. The environment must be a priority, but it can't be unless we make more of an effort to bring the younger generations with us to explore a truly sustainable future.

WHAT IS CLIMATE CHANGE?

CLIMATE CHANGE REFERS TO A FLUCTUATION IN LONGSTANDING RECORDED AVERAGES OF WEATHER PATTERNS. THESE CHANGES ARE ESCALATED BY GREENHOUSE GASES, OF WHICH HUMAN ACTIVITY PRODUCES SUBSTANTIAL EMISSIONS.

The climate is generally defined as the prevailing weather conditions over a specific region, or globally, looking at factors such as temperature, rainfall, and wind. Typically, average readings are taken over a 30-year period to assess the climate. "Climate change" refers to instances where this average alters, and generally when the changes continue over decades, centuries, or even longer, while "weather" is defined by conditions in a particular area over a shorter term of days and weeks. Climate change is accelerated by emissions of greenhouse gases, which become trapped in the Earth's atmosphere, absorbing and generating heat and warming the planet. These gases consist mainly of naturally occurring carbon dioxide, methane, nitrous oxide, and water vapor, as well as synthetic fluorinated gases. While most of the gases occur naturally on Earth, they are also produced in large quantities through human activities.

A report that was issued in 2021 by the IPCC (Intergovernmental Panel on Climate Change) attested to the fact that we are in a state of climate catastrophe, with a dramatic increase in the kind of events indicative of the early consequences of an increasingly unpredictable and altering climate. Soaring temperatures, destructive flooding, and ferocious forest fires are events that will continue to escalate unless we intervene rapidly. Though the COVID-19 pandemic saw a dip in emissions in 2020 to 2021 as the world stood still, this was not enough to decelerate our course for climate disaster. The report demonstrates how we need to employ momentum, innovation, and global cooperation to use our ever-narrowing window of opportunity to avoid a catastrophic global temperature increase of up to 5.4°F (3°C) in the next 50 years.

THE INTERGOVERNMENTAL PANEL ON CLIMATE CHANGE

The Intergovernmental Panel on Climate Change (IPCC) was established by the World Meteorological Organization and the United Nations Environment Program in 1988 to assess scientific information on climate change and to publish reports that summarize the science. In IPCC reports, climate change is referred to as a combination of both natural and human-induced factors. In other documentation, the term "climate change" is sometimes used to refer specifically to change caused by human activity.

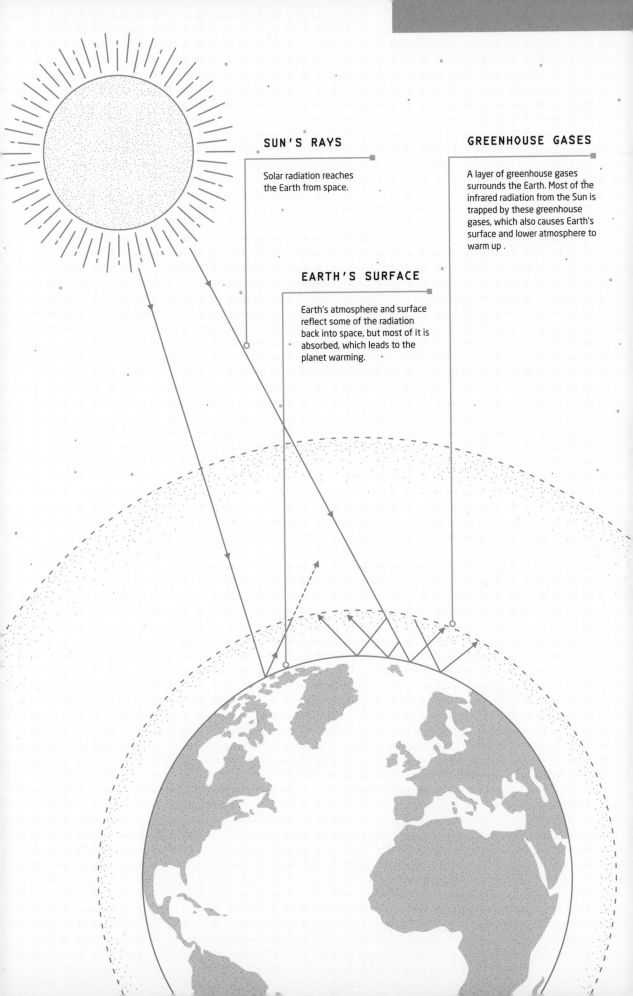

SUN'S RAYS

Solar radiation reaches
the Earth from space.

GREENHOUSE GASES

A layer of greenhouse gases
surrounds the Earth. Most of the
infrared radiation from the Sun is
trapped by these greenhouse
gases, which also causes Earth's
surface and lower atmosphere to
warm up .

EARTH'S SURFACE

Earth's atmosphere and surface
reflect some of the radiation
back into space, but most of it is
absorbed, which leads to the
planet warming.

Effects on the planet at 1.5 and 2°C
In 2022, the global warming level of approximately 1°C (1.8°F) was already causing damage, such as global heatwaves, ferocious wildfires, and devastating hurricanes. This graphic shows that for temperature increases of 1.5 and 2°C, the effects would become more widespread and extreme worldwide.

RISING TEMPERATURES

There have been natural shifts in Earth's climate since the birth of the planet. Over millennia, conditions have fluctuated substantially between colder glacial and warmer interglacial periods. There is irrefutable evidence to support the claim that human output directly affects the current global changes in our climate, largely due to the burning of fossil fuels that leach carbon dioxide into the atmosphere.

Temperatures in the atmosphere, greenhouse gas concentrations, and sea levels have all risen, while sea ice and snow levels have been steadily decreasing. There is now more than enough evidence to indicate that the climate has been warming since the arrival of the Industrial Revolution, in ways unparalleled to those seen even when looking back over millennia. Temperatures will continue to rise, bringing problematic consequences, with the outpouring of greenhouse gases.

It is estimated that if we continue to emit these gases at the present rate, there could be a temperature rise of 4.5–9°F (2.5–5°C) by the end

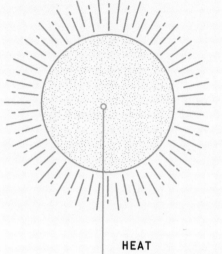

HEAT

+1.5°C 700 million people (9% of the world's population) would face extreme heat at least one in every 20 years.

+2°C 2 billion people (28% of the world's population) would face extreme heat at least one in every 20 years.

BIODIVERSITY

+1.5°C 8% of plants, 6% of insects, and 4% of vertebrates would be detrimentally affected.

+2°C 16% of plants, 18% of insects, and 8% of vertebrates would be detrimentally affected.

There is now more than enough recorded evidence to indicate that the climate has been warming since the arrival of the Industrial Revolution, in ways unparalleled to those seen even when looking back over millennia.

of the century. With a turn toward sustainable energy, this could drop to a rise of 0.4–3.1°F (0.25–1.75°C), but to achieve this, a considerable global effort will need to be adopted. Even with our best efforts, we are at a point now where we cannot completely alleviate the effects of climate change. We will need to adapt, finding new ways to build resilience and cope with threatening prospects worldwide.

EXTREME WEATHER

+1.5°C The risk of flooding would increase by 100%.

+2°C The risk of flooding would increase by 170%.

WATER AVAILABILITY

+1.5°C 350 million urban dwellers would experience severe drought conditions by 2100.

+2°C 410 million urban dwellers would experience severe drought conditions by 2100.

SEA-LEVEL RISE

+1.5°C A sea-level rise of 19in (48cm) by 2100 would impact 46 million people.

+2°C A sea-level rise of 22in (56cm) by 2100 would impact 49 million people.

GLOBAL CLIMATE CHANGE

WE ARE AT A CROSSROADS: IF A GLOBAL EFFORT IS MADE NOW TO SUBSTANTIALLY MINIMIZE GREENHOUSE GASES, THE RISE IN TEMPERATURES COULD BE ONLY TEMPORARY.

An interactive map is available that details the future climates of 530 cities across the world and links them to those that have their anticipated 2050 climate in the present day. London's climate could resemble that of Barcelona, a city 708 miles (1,140km) closer to the Equator, which would mean a 3.8°F (2.1°C) increase in the city's annual temperature forecast. Paris would probably resemble Canberra, while Milan could have the climate of present-day Dallas by 2050.

MITIGATION OF CLIMATE CHANGE

The IPCC's third report installment, which was issued on April 4, 2022, states that without immediate and deep reductions of emissions across all sectors, limiting global warming to 2.7°F (1.5°C) is beyond reach; but if the world's nations endeavor to substantially minimize greenhouse gases in the 2020s, then the overreach could be temporary, and temperatures would have the potential to revert by 2.7°F (1.5°C) by the end of the century.

To lower and restrict carbon dioxide accumulation in the atmosphere, it is expected that technologies such as carbon dioxide removal will need to be utilized, and the world must achieve net zero emissions by 2050.

"We are at a crossroads. The decisions we make now can secure a livable future. We have the tools and know-how required to limit warming," said IPCC Chair Hoesung Lee. "I am encouraged by climate action being taken in many countries. There are policies, regulations, and market instruments that are proving effective. If these are scaled up and applied more widely and equitably, they can support deep emissions reductions and stimulate innovation."

Key
- City with annual temperature rise
- Future city climate

SEATTLE
Annual temperature rise: **4.7°F (2.6°C)**
Future climate: **San Francisco**

WASHINGTON, DC
Annual temperature rise: **5.4°F (3°C)**
Future climate: **Nashville**

SANTIAGO
Annual temperature rise: **2°F (1.1°C)**
Future climate: **Nicosia**

SAO PAULO
Annual temperature rise: **2.5°F (1.4°C)**
Future climate: **Miami**

THE PARIS AGREEMENT AND COP26

At the climate change conference COP21 in Paris in 2015, an international treaty was signed with the goal of limiting global warming to below 3.6°F (2°C), ideally 2.7°F (1.5°C). This Paris Agreement could be seen as a pivotal point, accepting the necessity of action on climate change. But COP26 in Glasgow in 2021 failed to reassert the goals for 2030 that line up with a global warming limit of 2.7°F (1.5°C) and the pledge to hasten plans to phase out the use of coal.

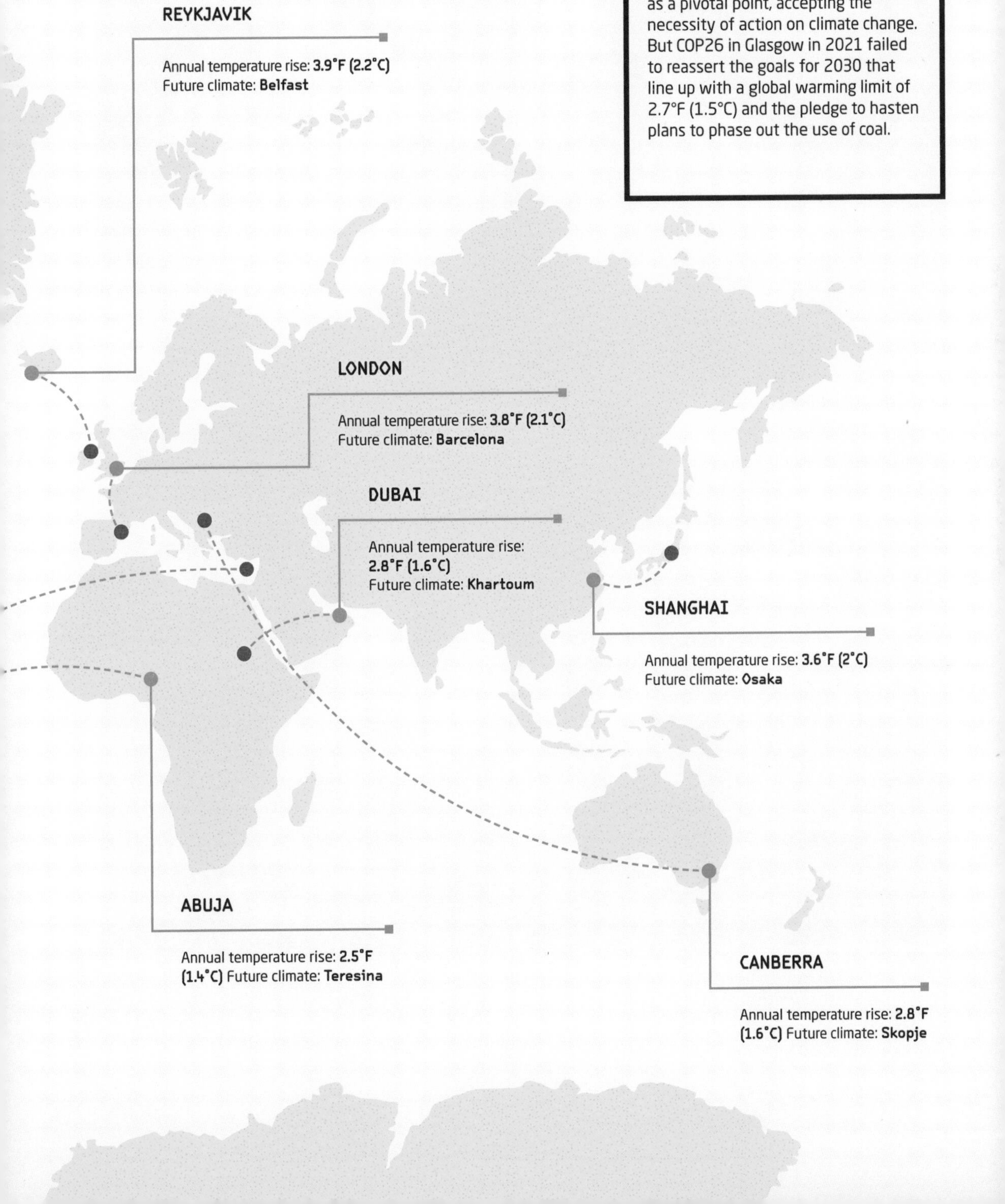

REYKJAVIK

Annual temperature rise: **3.9°F (2.2°C)**
Future climate: **Belfast**

LONDON

Annual temperature rise: **3.8°F (2.1°C)**
Future climate: **Barcelona**

DUBAI

Annual temperature rise: **2.8°F (1.6°C)**
Future climate: **Khartoum**

SHANGHAI

Annual temperature rise: **3.6°F (2°C)**
Future climate: **Osaka**

ABUJA

Annual temperature rise: **2.5°F (1.4°C)** Future climate: **Teresina**

CANBERRA

Annual temperature rise: **2.8°F (1.6°C)** Future climate: **Skopje**

The ability to grow warm-climate fruits outdoors in the UK, such as *Citrus lumia*, the pear lemon shown here, may sound like a bonus, but certain plants—both native and non-native—may not grow as well in our new climate, causing losses to the ecosystem.

WHAT DOES THIS MEAN FOR GARDENING?

GLOBAL WARMING WILL AFFECT OUR LIVES IN MANY WAYS, SOME OF WHICH WE CANNOT INFLUENCE. BUT HERE, WE SHALL EXPLORE WHAT THE CONSEQUENCES ARE FOR GARDENERS, LANDSCAPE DESIGNERS, AND THE HORTICULTURE INDUSTRY AND HOW GARDENS CAN BE DESIGNED SO THEY ARE RESILIENT TO THE PREDICTED EFFECTS.

The world is made up of varied landscapes and habitats, for example polar regions, tundra, evergreen forests, seasonal forests, grasslands, deserts, tropical rainforests, oceans, and the built environment (meaning towns, cities, and other human architecture). Climate change is expected to affect every country across the globe, but the impact will not be equal due to social, political, geographic, and climatic conditions. This book cannot provide specific information for gardening in worldwide environments; however, it offers guidelines, principles, ideas, and inspiration that can be adapted to a number of different contexts to help mitigate the negative impacts of climate change and make the most of the opportunities a warming climate presents.

LOCAL CHANGES

I live in the UK, which is in a temperate region, where climate scientists predict that we can expect to experience warmer, wetter winters and hotter, drier summers, with frost potentially being a thing of the past. In some ways, this doesn't sound too bad, as it presents the opportunity of cultivating a wider array of exotic and unusual plants. The idea of being able to grow avocados, pomegranates, mangoes, and citrus fruits in our gardens and allotments probably sounds enticing to most British gardeners. However, the planet's ecosystems are in fine balance, and as climate change takes effect, we need to consider the risks and the loss of plants that we might mourn alongside the opportunities.

RESTORING ECOSYSTEMS

"Healthy ecosystems are more resilient to climate change and provide life-critical services such as food and clean water," said IPCC Working Group II co-chair professor Hans-Otto Pörtner in February 2022. "By restoring degraded ecosystems and effectively and equitably conserving 30 to 50 percent of Earth's land, freshwater, and ocean habitats, society can benefit from nature's capacity to absorb and store carbon, and we can accelerate progress toward sustainable development, but adequate finance and political support are essential."

HOTHOUSE PROJECT

The Hothouse, a collaboration between myself and Je,
was commissioned by developer Lendlease as a landmark
project for the London Design Festival 2020.

JE AHN is an architect and founder of design practice Studio Weave in London. The Hackney-based studio creates pioneering designs for pubic and private clients with a focus on building community, championing sustainable practice, and initiating collaborations across disciplines.

"

WHAT INSPIRED THE DESIGN FOR THE HOTHOUSE? IT'S A BEAUTIFUL STRUCTURE WITH AN ALLURING ELEMENT OF PLAYFULNESS IN THE DESIGN.

I feel architecture should offer delight, and garden design is similar—something that gives us comfort and joy, seeing ourselves as not separate from nature but a part of it.

The Hothouse design comes from the context of the site, Lee Valley, where the landscape has been used for food production for generations. The controlled environment of the hothouse building gives the opportunity to cultivate plants that won't necessarily grow or be productive in the current climate in this country.

I love the idea of having a more Mediterranean climate in the UK, but on the flip side, it is a scary thought that the climate is changing so rapidly that scientists predict that we may see avocado and citrus trees as common plants in London in the near future. I thought this was an interesting way to transmit a message on the changing climate.

HOW IMPORTANT DO YOU THINK THE LANDSCAPE IS IN THE PUBLIC REALM, AND HOW CAN WE IMPROVE THE DIALOGUE BETWEEN LANDSCAPE AND THE BUILT ENVIRONMENT?

I don't see a distinction between designing buildings and designing for land around them. Some rebalancing is needed—we went through an era where design was too human-centric, and we need to change to nature first, with humans and nature in harmony.

HOW ARE YOU DESIGNING CLIMATE RESILIENCE INTO YOUR WORK, AND HAS THIS CHANGED IN THE TIME YOU HAVE BEEN PRACTICING?

My attitude has always been that a building is something we create to protect ourselves from certain environments, but while we're doing that, we also have to protect our habitat—the planet itself. On the practical side, it was a lot harder 10 years ago to find information or products seeking to reduce carbon footprint. While this is increasingly easy, there are still regulations that need to be adapted to encourage sustainable use of materials, how labor is organized, and how we transport materials.

RISKS AND OPPORTUNITIES

There are several main climate issues facing gardeners and landscape designers in the UK and other temperate regions. Flooding and heavy rainfall causes waterlogged soil and damages plants; it can also cause or worsen soil erosion, as can strong winds, which have the capacity to bring down mature trees, too. Warmer winters could spell an increase in diseases and pests, without the cold to eliminate them. Unpredictable frosts may kill off plants blooming earlier in milder winters, while hotter, drier summers will bring heat stress and parched soil, meaning that the need for water will escalate.

KEY OPPORTUNITIES

These issues can also create opportunities, with the possibility of cultivating a more diverse range of species over a longer growing season. Floodwater can be accommodated within green spaces and retained for irrigation during the drier months, while green infrastructure offers cooling potential, and planting schemes can be designed to be adaptable and less reliant on input of resources.

BIOPHILIC DESIGN

Psychoanalyst Erich Fromm first introduced the word "biophilia" in his 1973 book *The Anatomy of Human Destructiveness*. He described it as the "passionate love of life and of all that is alive . . . whether in a person, a plant, an idea, or a social group."

Biophilic design is employed by architects and designers to increase connectivity to the natural world in built environments at both residential and city scale. It is argued that biophilic design and an increased connection to nature has health, environmental, and economic benefits. Initiatives can be as small as bringing cut flowers into the home or as large as mass tree plantings or urban greening plans.

[Above] Nigel Dunnett, professor of landscape architecture at Sheffield University and landscape designer, uses logs as sculptural wave forms in his own garden, providing habitats as well as aesthetic structures.

[Left] Charred logs sweep through the landscape in the Yeo Valley Organic Garden at RHS Chelsea Flower Show 2021. Such logs eventually break down, adding charcoal to the soil to hold nutrients and water.

01

[01] In the Perennial Sanctuary Garden, exhibited at RHS Hampton Court Flower Show in 2017, I used minimal hard landscaping and championed swathes of uplifting planting to create an immersive, peaceful escape. [02] Small multistem trees, such as this *Amelanchier lamarckii*, are a good option for small gardens, as their light canopy allows dappled light to filter through. [03] *Crataegus monogyna* is a typical hedgerow plant in the UK, but "pruned up" to reveal the multistem form, it can be a beautiful specimen tree. [04] Timber composting bays, with a roof designed to be covered in climbing plants, create an aesthetically pleasing compost area.

02

03

KEY ACTIONS FOR GARDENERS

CONSIDERING HOW WE OPTIMIZE OUR OUTSIDE SPACE AND MAKING SUSTAINABLE CHOICES CAN HAVE A HUGE IMPACT IN SUPPORTING OUR ECOSYSTEMS AND INCREASING THE SUSTAINABILITY OF OUR GARDENS.

INCLUDE TREES

There is nearly always a suitable tree for any garden; choose species that are able to deal with local climatic conditions and will cope with the future changes to the climate, too. Mitigate the loss of any trees with at least one, but preferably multiple, replacements, as they draw carbon out of the air. As it is an important habitat for many species, including rare invertebrates, dead wood is best left in the landscape—with a bit of creative thinking, it can be aesthetically pleasing, too.

REDUCE HARD LANDSCAPING

While gardens need hard surfaces for practical accessibility, areas of hard materials such as paving don't need to be impermeable deserts. For example, leaving planted channels between slabs or using permeable materials such as gravel can add to the aesthetic interest of the space, as well as reducing the risk of flooding.

PRODUCE COMPOST

Every 2¼lb (1kg) of site-made compost typically saves 3½oz (100g) of carbon dioxide emissions, which could add up to more than 11¼lb (5.1kg) carbon saved per gardener every year. Although it doesn't usually represent the most beautiful space, compost production is key to a sustainable, circular approach where the aim is that nothing is sent to landfills. With forethought, the composting area can be screened creatively. There are also discreet and compact "off-the-shelf" composting units for small spaces. These take up little room and can compost at accelerated rates due to their innovative designs.

04

[01] Solar panels on a green roof provide renewable energy. [02] Pioneering green architect Emilio Ambasz transposed a 120,000sq yd (100,000sq m) park in the city center onto 15 stepped terraces of the ACROS Fukuoka Prefectural International Hall, creating a stunning roof park and utilizing roof space that would otherwise lie empty. [03] Productive beds can be incorporated in many different spaces, and growing food can bring us closer to nature. Here, an allotment on the roof of the Queen Elizabeth Hall, South Bank, London, provides food for the center's cafés and restaurants.

02

01

03

04

[04] At Stylus, 116 Old Street, London, landscape designer John Davies' primary aim was to maximize the biodiversity of the roof area to increase the ecological impact on the local environment. An intensive green roof system supports a mix of trees, shrubs, perennials, and grasses, combined with 48sq yd (40sq m) of green walls designed in collaboration with Tapestry Vertical Gardens, a green wall specialist. [05] Seedheads and grasses provide beautiful interest in the fall and winter months, as demonstrated here by Nigel Dunnett's planting at the Barbican Centre, London.

USE RENEWABLE TECHNOLOGIES

Reduce your reliance on fossil fuels and incorporate renewable technologies where climatic conditions allow, for example solar panels; solar lighting; wind power; and hydroelectric, ground- and air-sourced heating technologies.

THINK ABOUT GREENING ON ALL PLANES

Vertical surfaces such as fences and walls can be greened with climbing plants or green wall technologies, offering a range of benefits that include habitats, food, and shelter for animals and invertebrates. They can also provide insulation for buildings.

ADD GREEN ROOFS

Green roof systems can be incorporated into any structures—sheds, garages, bin stores—with forethought and planning. This will increase biodiversity and can sequester up to ¾lb per 1¼sq yd (0.375kg carbon per sq m) per year. They also insulate the internal spaces beneath them and can increase the life of the roof membranes. For retro-fitting projects, ensure that the structure is capable of taking the increased weight; consult a structural engineer if you are in doubt.

INCLUDE PRODUCTIVE PLANTS

You could opt for a formal productive area, with raised beds; a more integrated approach, with edimentals (ornamental edibles) incorporated into the wider planting; or a "food forest" approach, where interlinked species of productive plants and trees sustainably coexist. Planning for food production can be educational, particularly for children, and deepens our connection with nature. It is rewarding, and the end result is delicious, too!

DESIGN SEASONAL PLANTING AREAS

Successional planting design, where different species of plants flower throughout the year and succeed each other, can mean that cut flowers, foliage, and seedheads are available for use year-round. Cut flowers and foliage bring nature inside and can save up to 17½lb (7.9kg) carbon per bunch compared with buying imported or commercially produced bunches.

05

The depletion of pollinators and declining soil health has a devastating effect on the food chain and delicate global ecosystems. Sir Robert Watson, who is chair of the Intergovernmental Science-Policy Platform on Biodiversity and Ecosystem Services (IPBES), states that there is overwhelming evidence that "the health of ecosystems on which we and all other species depend is deteriorating more rapidly than ever. We are eroding the very foundations of our economies, livelihoods, food security, health, and quality of life worldwide." Urgent and sustained action is required to remedy the biodiversity crisis across all activities of the economy.

THE BIODIVERSITY CRISIS

ALONGSIDE THE CLIMATE EMERGENCY IS THE BIODIVERSITY CRISIS, WHICH IS EQUALLY URGENT. WE ARE SEEING A DECLINE IN AND EXTINCTIONS OF WILD AND CULTIVATED SPECIES WORLDWIDE.

MAP LOCAL BIODIVERSITY

If you live in the UK, you can help map the biodiversity of garden plants by adding the plants in your garden to RHS My Garden online (rhs.org.uk/my-garden). The RHS has information and resources that will help you grow and conserve this important biodiversity for future generations to enjoy. Species identification apps are also available worldwide that enable anyone with a smartphone to identify and learn about the plants in their garden or local area.

INSECT ARMAGEDDON

Entomologists are warning us of the disastrous effect environmental pressures are having on the essential insect population. A warming planet, overzealous usage of pesticides, pollution (of light, soil, and air), and loss of habitat are some of the factors in a dangerous concoction threatening insect life. The crucial role insects play within our ecosystem cannot be overestimated: they are the tiny workers holding the rest of us up. Without them, we would be plunged into ecological pandemonium.

Professor Dave Goulson of Sussex University in the UK states: "Insects make up about two-thirds of all life on Earth [but] there has been some kind of horrific decline. We appear to be making vast tracts of land inhospitable to most forms of life, and are currently on course for ecological Armageddon. If we lose the insects, then everything is going to collapse."

As gardeners, we can support insects in many ways, providing habitats, food sources, cover, and protection and avoiding the use of harmful and indiscriminate chemical pesticides.

[Top] You may have noticed that there are not nearly as many insects splattered on your car after driving as there used to be. [Left] Bees killed by the use of agricultural pesticides.

INCLUDE INSECT HABITATS

Invertebrate and insect decline is a global crisis driven by unsustainable practices. We need to consider insects in our planning, designing their habitats into the gardens. A garden designed for diverse invertebrate life will also be full of biodiverse plant life: one sustains the other.

DESIGN FOR WILDLIFE

Larger wild animals, such as birds and mammals, also need our help. Habitat loss is an increasing global problem due to urbanization: local wildlife is being forced out. We can provide food and shelter in our gardens and share these spaces with wild species. Our gardens are not just for us.

GARDEN WITHOUT TOXIC CHEMICALS

Pesticides, fungicides, and weedkillers are not specific to the pests, pathogens, and weeds that users are targeting. Beneficial pollinating insects can be killed by pesticides, and poisoned slugs can be eaten by wild animals and pets, unintentionally killing them. Adopting good practice in cultivation, cultivar selection, and garden hygiene—and encouraging natural enemies—reduces pest, disease, and weed problems and helps biodiversity. Using sustainably produced fertilizers such as organic seaweed feed, homemade comfrey tea, or organic farmyard manure further avoids environmental damage.

PLANT SUSTAINABLE SCHEMES

"Right plant, right place," the adage coined by visionary gardener Beth Chatto, is increasingly important. Today, it refers not only to current conditions, but to future conditions and unpredictable weather events. Well-designed plant communities can adapt to local climate events, such as flooding or drought, needing little human intervention. Victorian-style bedding plantings, expansive lawns, and regularly mown roundabouts and roadside verges need to be relegated to history.

INCLUDE NATURAL WATER

Natural ponds and small water features provide an extra habitat in gardens, significantly enhancing biodiversity. These need to be free of harmful chemicals such as chlorine and bromine and should ideally include planting as shelter for wildlife, which also oxygenates the water, keeping it healthy.

CONSIDER ALTERNATIVES TO LAWNS

Traditional mown green lawns, which are limited to a few species of turf grasses, could be described as "green deserts" with little ecological value. By mowing less, you will allow flowering species to provide food for pollinators. Consider alternatives to a lawn where it is not possible to keep it in good condition without constant input of resources, such as water and fertilizers.

01

BUILDING IN BIODIVERSITY

PLACING BIODIVERSITY AT THE FOREFRONT OF OUR GARDENING CHOICES WILL HELP PROTECT AND SUPPORT AN ESSENTIAL PART OF OUR ECOSYSTEM, AS WELL AS CREATING A BEAUTIFUL, THRIVING GARDEN FULL OF LIFE.

[01] Including insect habitats will help support our dwindling and essential invertebrate and insect populations. [02] Natural ponds and small water features provide an extra habitat for biodiversity, and frogs and toads are a natural form of pest control. [03] Using nontoxic ways to manage your garden means a safe environment for wildlife, and will encourage natural pest control. Comfrey (*Symphytum officinale*) can be used to make an organic fertilizer (see pages **126–127**).

02

03

04

05

06

[04] Sustainable planting schemes with a mix of native and non-native plants provide a beautiful, diverse habitat, as demonstrated here by Professor James Hitchmough at RHS Garden Wisley, UK. [05] Natural water features provide peaceful sounds and can be chemical free, with natural filtration systems.
[06] Meadow planting is a great alternative to a lawn and requires less maintenance. There are meadow mat products that are laid like turf, yielding quick, reliable results.

Thousands of ancient olive trees in Italy,
destroyed by *Xylella fastidiosa*.

BIOSECURITY THREATS

THE INTRODUCTION OF PESTS AND DISEASES CAN SPELL DISASTER FOR NATIVE PLANTS, COMPOUNDED BY UNSUSTAINABLE HORTICULTURAL PRACTICES AND CLIMATE CHANGE.

Threats to plants can come in the form of pests, diseases, and invasive non-native plants. The introduction of plants for aesthetic or commercial reasons can sometimes spell disaster for native species. This issue can be compounded by the effects of climate change, which can act in favor of aggressive, adaptable, non-native plants and unfavorably for sensitive native species. Horticulture is often regarded as the main entry point for these non-native species, which have usually been introduced for their ornamental properties. Legislative developments around the world now recognize this, with the introduction of programs aimed at managing non-native invasive plant species such as Japanese knotweed and giant hogweed, pests such as Asian hornets and American bullfrogs, and diseases such as Dutch elm disease and horse chestnut bleeding canker.

The shift in horticultural rhythms is one way in which gardeners can see a noticeable effect, especially at the turn of the seasons, noting a change in the emergence of new leaves, the early appearance of flowers, or tree foliage beginning to change hue. The timing of these occurrences is unequivocally related to the changing climate and can affect biosecurity, too—for example, pests may no longer be killed off by cold weather, and invasive species may be able to thrive in warmer, wetter, or dryer climates. A resilient garden is one that is resilient to pests and diseases, as well as to climate change.

> The introduction of plants for aesthetic or commercial reasons can spell disaster for native species. This can be compounded by the effects of climate change, which can act in favor of aggressive, adaptable, non-native plants and unfavorably for sensitive native species.

XYLELLA FASTIDIOSA

An example of a bacterial disease that has damaging effects on a wide range of plants is *Xylella fastidiosa*, which is spread solely by xylem sap-feeding insects. There have been outbreaks of this disease in many parts of Europe, with the decimation of thousands of olive trees in Italy, including ancient groves. As the disease causes afflictions such as leaf scorch, wilting, dieback, and plant death, the UK government and horticultural industry have understandable anxieties over the risk of it being introduced to the environment by means of imported contaminated plants. Stringent measures are being executed in an attempt to keep *Xylella* from entering the UK. A scheme has been initiated by Natural England (NE) to prevent and manage invasive non-native species such as this.

CHAPTER THREE

ANALYZING YOUR SITE

SITE ANALYSIS

IT IS ESSENTIAL TO UNDERSTAND THE SPECIFIC CONDITIONS OF YOUR GARDEN IN ORDER TO DESIGN A RESILIENT AND SUSTAINABLE LANDSCAPE.

When designing a resilient and sustainable garden, it is important that you acquire a good understanding of the climatic conditions of your site and how they will affect it in both the short term and the future. Planning for adaptability at the outset is important to ensure resilience long term. This ethos needs to run through the entire design, from what happens on and beneath the ground (topsoils, subsoils, drainage, and even subbase materials), through to the surface finishes (paving, decking, cladding, and mulches), and into planting and tree selection, ensuring that all plants are suitable for the site long term. Ultimately, the aim is to provide multiple benefits for our gardens, ourselves, and the wider environments around us.

Understanding soil conditions is integral to designing a planting scheme that will thrive. A trial pit reveals the below-ground conditions, showing the soil profile (see pages 66–67).

LOCATION

WHERE IS YOUR SITE LOCATED AND WHAT ARE THE ASSOCIATED CLIMATIC CONDITIONS THAT WILL AFFECT WHAT YOU CAN GROW?

The location can dramatically affect the suitability and sustainability of your garden's plants and materials. For example, a coastal garden will often have to cope with high winds and may be exposed to high levels of salt, which can be corrosive and damaging to plants that aren't adapted to these conditions. City gardens may be affected by contaminated soils, pollution, raised temperatures from an urban heat island, and wind tunnels caused by tall buildings. Gardens may also be located in floodplains (or potential floodplains in the future), deserts, mountainous regions, or forests. Each type of location will have unique characteristics and a microclimate that will need to be assessed.

[Top] My design for the Yard House city garden is situated within a courtyard, so it is very sheltered. This garden is close to a busy main street, so it has to contend with high pollution levels and urban temperatures.
[Above] Coastal gardens can get battered by strong winds and high levels of salt from the sea, so hardy shrubs and trees are good choices. Look at what is growing well locally for inspiration.

URBAN HEAT ISLANDS

Cities and other built-up urban sprawls can considerably affect the environment as human intervention creates distinctive changes in both weather and climate. The combination of an intense concentration of towering buildings, networks of roads, and concrete and glass structures can create complex temperature, rain, wind, and atmosphere formations. The placement of tall buildings can cause wind tunnels, while impermeable surfaces channel water and increase the risk of flooding. Air quality is compromised by pollution from invisible particles expelled by traffic and industry. The urban heat island effect can cause temperatures in cities to rise by up to 9°F (5°C), which heightens the intensity of heatwaves.

MICROCLIMATE

This term refers to the climate of a small area, especially one that differs from the climate of the surrounding area—for example, an urban light-well or a walled garden.

SUBURBS

Areas with more built structures will absorb more heat and reradiate it back into the atmosphere, increasing the temperature.

RURAL AREAS

The plants and trees in rural areas absorb far less heat than the dark, man-made materials that are more prevalent in urban environments.

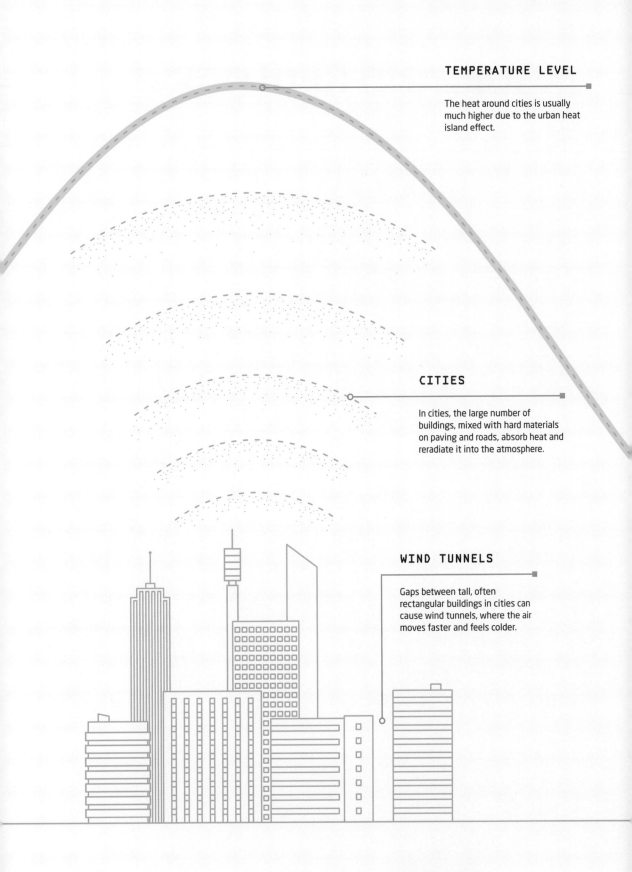

TEMPERATURE LEVEL

The heat around cities is usually much higher due to the urban heat island effect.

CITIES

In cities, the large number of buildings, mixed with hard materials on paving and roads, absorb heat and reradiate it into the atmosphere.

WIND TUNNELS

Gaps between tall, often rectangular buildings in cities can cause wind tunnels, where the air moves faster and feels colder.

SOIL AND GEOLOGY

WHAT IS THE MAKE-UP OF THE EXISTING SOIL IN YOUR GARDEN? DO YOU HAVE A SUFFICIENT DEPTH OF TOPSOIL, AND WILL IT BE AFFECTED BY EROSION?

Understanding your soil is key to knowing what will grow successfully on the site; while some plants are tolerant of a range of conditions, others are not, so you need to know whether yours is light and sandy, heavy clay, or a loamy soil (see pages 68–69). You may have a deep layer of topsoil, or it may be scarce or even nonexistent. Soil erosion is a risk on exposed sites on steep slopes, and it may be worsened by the effects of climate change, such as heavy rainfall, flash flooding, or baking heat.

Existing soils can be improved by adding organic matter, such as homemade compost. If the condition is really poor, or if the soil is contaminated, you can import topsoil—but bear in mind that this isn't always the most sustainable practice. Check that the soil supplier complies with local laws and standards for sustainability and that the soil has been properly screened for contaminants. If this information is vague, you may prefer to look for a more reputable supplier who is transparent about their sources and processes of production.

SOIL MAPS

Consulting soil maps is a good way to learn about the conditions of your site. Geographical maps that break down the soil type and geology of an area are available online, often provided as free resources from universities. You can investigate further by digging trial pits; testing by hand; or engaging a soil expert to analyze the makeup, pH, and condition of the soil. In the UK, the RHS offers a soil analysis service, which examines soil texture, pH, organic matter content, and the presence of three major plant nutrients: potassium, phosphorus, and magnesium.

Existing soils can be improved by adding organic matter, such as homemade compost. If the condition is really poor, or if the soil is contaminated, you can import topsoil—but bear in mind that this isn't always the most sustainable practice.

TOPSOIL

The type of topsoil you buy is also important to consider. A fertile, moisture-retentive, humus-rich loam would not be suitable for a planting of drought-tolerant species inspired by Mediterranean landscapes, for example: most plants from that region will not tolerate damp soils and need a more free-draining medium. A good starting point is to research where the plants you have in mind grow in the wild and what type of soil conditions they thrive in. Telling topsoil suppliers about the planting you hope to achieve will allow them to recommend suitable soil blends for your garden.

SOIL HORIZONS

Soil is formed in layers, and individual layers are referred to as soil horizons. These make up the soil profile. In order to discover the soil profile of a site, a pit is dug to reveal a vertical cross-section.

ORGANIC LAYER

This layer is dark black-brown, undecomposed at the top and more decomposed at the bottom. The organic layer can be deep, shallow, or even absent in some soils.

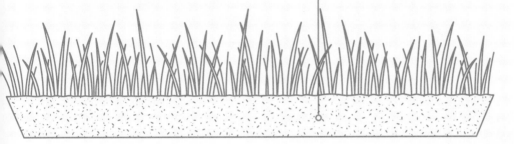

TOPSOIL

The topsoil is made up of decayed organic matter (humus) and a combination of sand, silt, and clay. It is dark brown in color, as it contains organic matter with some minerals.

SUBSOIL

Subsoil is lighter than topsoil due to lower humus and higher mineral content. It is more rigid and compact than the topsoil. Substances move down from the topsoil layer and accumulate in the subsoil.

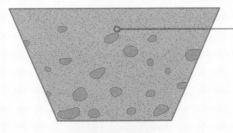

PARENT ROCK

The parent rock layer is made of broken-up bedrock, making it hard and stony. It is devoid of organic matter. Plant roots do not extend into this layer. This is the transition between the inner rock layer of the earth and the upper layers of soil.

BEDROCK

The bedrock is hard and compact and consists of unweathered igneous, sedimentary, and metamorphic rocks. This largely comprises continuous masses rather than smaller rocks.

067

SOIL COMPOSITION

Soil is made up of varying proportions of inorganic particles of many different sizes. The combination of size and proportion determines some of the properties of the soil.

Permeable soils allow water to move freely through their structures, as the spaces between the particles are large and well connected. Sandy and silty soils display these characteristics and are often referred to as "light." They hold less water and don't become waterlogged or "heavy," as soils with a high clay content do.

Other soils have numerous small spaces that retain water. Clay, for example, is made up of numerous small particles, and this makes the soil "heavier," meaning it has a denser structure that compacts easily.

A mixture of grain sizes is referred to as a "loam." Measuring the percentage of sand, silt, and clay allows soil scientists to describe the soil type.

CHALKY SOIL

Soil with particles larger than $\frac{1}{16}$in (2mm) is classified as stony. Chalky soils are often very stony and are also made up of calcium carbonate, or lime, making them alkaline and difficult to keep fertile.

CLAY SOIL

Also known as heavy soils, clay soils have particles of less than 0.002mm, and they are composed of more than 25 percent clay. Nutrients bind to the clay minerals in the soil, which makes this soil type very fertile. However, the spaces between the clay particles are tiny, so clay soil holds water, drains slowly, and is easily compacted if it is trodden on when wet. It also takes a while to warm up during the hotter months, but once it has done so, it can then bake to a hard consistency with visible cracks.

LOAM

A loamy soil combines different soil types, which avoids the extreme characteristics of each. Made up of clay, sand, and silt, loams are fertile, free-draining, and easy to work. You can buy loam that is predominantly clay or sand, depending on your planting scheme.

SANDY SOIL

The particles of sand are defined as 0.05 to 2mm. Also known as light soils, sandy soils have a high proportion of sand and very little clay, meaning water drains through them easily, and they warm up more quickly than soils with a higher proportion of clay. However, the water washing through the particles can remove nutrients, leaving sandy soils dry, low in nutrients, and acidic.

SILT SOIL

This type of soil has particles from 0.002 to 0.05mm in size. It is fertile, drains well, and also holds moisture well, but a disadvantage is that it is easily compacted in wet weather.

SOIL MICROORGANISMS

All soil teems with microorganisms, such as fungi, algae, and bacteria. They help supply plants with the minerals and nutrients that are crucial for keeping them healthy, as well as enriching the soil.

SOIL TYPES

YOUR GARDEN MAY HAVE A MIXTURE OF SOIL TYPES. EACH TYPE HAS DIFFERENT CHARACTERISTICS, WHICH PARTLY DEPEND ON THE SIZE OF THE PARTICLES WITHIN IT. SOIL CAN BE DIFFICULT TO ANALYZE WITHOUT PROFESSIONAL ASSESSMENT, BUT HERE IS SOME GUIDANCE.

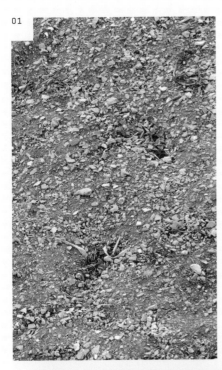

01

02

[01] Chalky soil is very alkaline and supports plants that are drought tolerant and like nutrient-poor soil. [02] Clay soils are very moisture retentive and often rich in nutrients.

03

04

05

[03] Loam is a mixture of clay, sand, and silt that avoids the extremes of other soils. Loam is generally well drained, fertile, and easy to work with. [04] Sandy soils are often very acidic, quick to drain, and quick to dry out. [05] Silt soils are fairly rare to find in a garden. They are usually fertile, fairly well drained, and hold more moisture than sandy soils but are easily compacted. Silt soils are prone to washing away and being eroded by wind if they are left exposed without plant cover or a surface mulch.

TESTING YOUR SOIL

IT'S USEFUL TO KNOW WHERE THE SOIL IN YOUR GARDEN SITS ON THE PH SCALE OF ACIDITY/ALKALINITY, AS THIS WILL INDICATE THE TYPES OF PLANTS THAT WILL STRUGGLE OR THRIVE.

It is a good idea to test the soil before you start designing your plot so that you don't waste money on plants that won't grow well. If you already have an established garden but have had a run of failed crops and yellowing leaves, testing your soil might determine the cause.

The pH scale runs from 1 to 14. If the pH level of your soil is below 7, it is acidic; if it is above 7, it is alkaline (rich in lime and chalk). A pH level of 7 is neutral, which is best for most plants. A basic way of checking the lime levels of your soil at home is to add vinegar to a sample of soil; if it fizzes, this indicates the presence of calcium carbonate (chalk). You can buy inexpensive kits for testing pH levels at most garden centers, but for more specific results, send a sample of your soil to a laboratory for analysis. Bear in mind that if you have added lime, fertilizer, or organic matter to your soil within the last three months, this will affect the results.

If your soil is acidic, you can add lime to balance out the pH levels. Alternatively, if it is alkaline, you can balance it by adding acidifying materials to neutralize the pH, such as sulfur dust or granules. However, it takes a lot of additives to cause a significant change in pH. This has sustainability implications, and the soil will soon revert to type, so it's best to plant species that are suited to your existing soil.

HOW TO PREVENT SOIL EROSION

The effects of climate change can lead to soil erosion, which is where the structure of the soil is degraded; it may be washed away by flooding, displaced by high winds, and dehydrated by high temperatures. By encouraging the health of microorganisms in the soil, gardeners help it build resilience against these challenges. Here are some tips:

- Maintain a healthy level of plant cover in the soil all year round.
- Mulch to cover and protect the soil. Types of mulch used worldwide can include stone aggregate, wood chips, or bark mulch.
- In heavily trafficked areas, and where planting is difficult to establish and maintain—such as under the canopy of evergreen trees or shrubs—use mulches to cover and protect the soil.
- Use products such as geotextile materials and meshes to help retain the soil. Planting can be done through the mesh—if it is made of biodegradable material such as coir or jute, it will degrade as the plants become established.
- Address areas vulnerable to stormwater runoff with solutions such as swales (see p.136), which can settle and dissipate water, preventing erosion.

PH 3.0-5.0

- Very acidic soil
- Most plant nutrients—particularly calcium, potassium, magnesium, and copper—become more soluble under very acid conditions and are easily washed away.
- Below pH 5.1, most phosphates are locked up and unavailable to plants.
- Bacteria cannot rot organic matter below pH 4.7, resulting in fewer nutrients available to plants.
- Action: Add lime to raise the pH to above 5.0. This can also help break up acid clay soils.

PH 5.1-6.0

- Acidic soil
- Ideal for ericaceous (lime-hating) plants, such as rhododendrons, camellias, and heathers.
- Action: Add lime only if other plants are struggling.

PH 6.1-7.0

- Moderately acidic soil
- A pH of 6.5 is the best general-purpose pH level for gardens, allowing a wide range of plants to grow except those that hate lime.
- The availability of major nutrients is at its highest, and bacterial and earthworm activity is also optimum at this pH.
- Action: No action needed.

PH 7.1-8.0

- Alkaline soil
- Phosphorus availability decreases.
- Iron and manganese become less available, leading to lime-induced chlorosis.
- An advantage is that clubroot disease, which affects brassicas (cabbage family crops), is reduced.
- Action: Sulfur, iron sulfate, and other acidifying agents can be added to reduce pH. Clay soils often need large amounts of acidifying material, and soils with high levels of chalk or lime are not usually treatable.

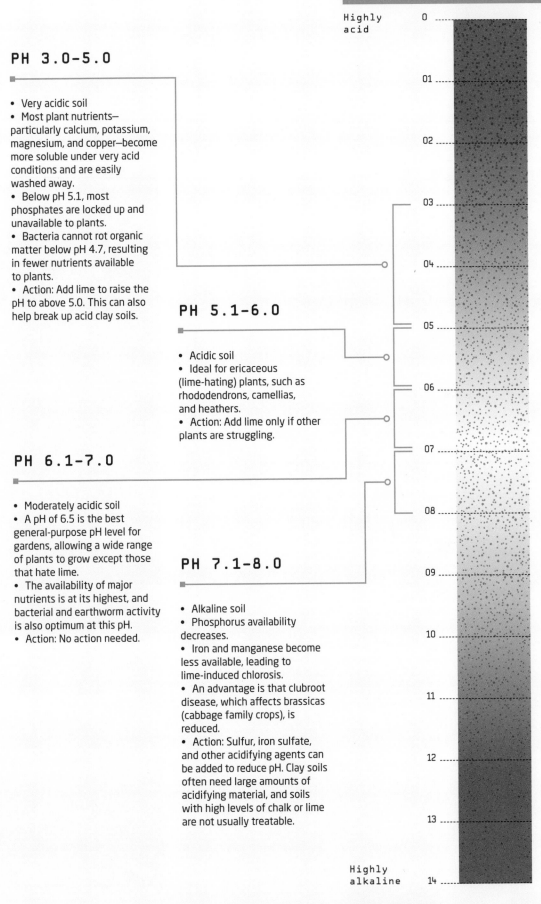

Highly acid

0
01
02
03
04
05
06
07
08
09
10
11
12
13
Highly alkaline   14

PLANTS

TO DETERMINE WHICH PLANTS WILL GROW SUCCESSFULLY IN YOUR GARDEN, LOOK AT THE WIDER NATURAL ENVIRONMENT TO DISCOVER SPECIES THAT ARE THRIVING NEARBY.

One of the best ways of analyzing what will grow successfully in a garden is to look at what else is thriving locally. Spend time gathering photographs, articles, and scientific reports on local nature reserves, parks, or botanical gardens; you can then use this data to guide your planting process. This approach is particularly important when you're designing and maintaining sustainable planting schemes. Forcing plants to grow where they won't thrive is never going to be sustainable, as huge amounts of time and resources will be needed to keep them going in conditions to which they aren't naturally suited.

In the wild, plants thrive in sustainable communities without any human input such as watering, pruning, mowing, or tidying. However, it is worth noting that natural processes, such as wildfires or grazing by deer, often replicate these processes. Many wild species can also work well in a garden setting. Consider the site's existing conditions and those it is expected to experience in the future and add adaptable plants that will be able to deal with those conditions, increasing the resilience of your garden.

[Top] Warm temperatures and steady rains lead to an explosion of color in the Anza-Borrego desert: a super bloom of California poppies and other wildflowers blankets the hills.
[Right] The stunning colors of the super bloom of spring flowers on the Temblor Mountain range in California draws visitors from miles around.

"A SITE CAN BE CHANGED TO FIT A PLANT;
BUT ONLY WHEN A PLANT FITS A SITE WILL
YOUR PLANTING TRULY BE SELF-SUSTAINING."

THOMAS RAINER, PLANTING IN A POST-WILD WORLD

NATIVE OR NON-NATIVE PLANTS?

A CONSIDERED MIX OF NATIVE AND NON-NATIVE PLANTING COULD BE THE ANSWER TO MITIGATING THE ISSUES CAUSED BY CLIMATE CHANGE, PROVIDING A RESILIENT, RICH, AND DIVERSE ECOSYSTEM.

Exotic, non-native landscapes are often alluring. Botanical gardens and greenhouses are popular places to visit, but the non-native plants that grow within bring with them issues of culture and context and potentially invasive species, pests that have no local predators, and devastating diseases.

Native-only planting schemes are also an attractive idea, but they often don't provide the hit of color or sustained interest that non-native or cultivated varieties can bring. Native plants may also have shorter flowering seasons, and, in a changing climate, non-native varieties may be better suited to their new conditions. Perhaps the answer is that we should plant a mix: cultivated "wild" environments.

Both private gardens and public parks can demonstrate the role that non-native plants play alongside native species, dramatically extending the flowering season. Non-native plants can also offer food for pollinators where native species affected by climate change are flowering too early or declining in heat or drought. Careful and sensitive design, combining native and non-native species, can ensure that biodiverse ecosystems are provided.

WILD VS. CULTIVATED PLANTS

The word "cultivar" is derived from the description "cultivated variety." Cultivar names are assigned to plants that are a variant within a species or that have been formed via hybridization, where two botanically distinct plants are cross-bred to produce something new. The names are denoted using single quotation marks and are not presented in italics, which differentiates them from botanical names.

Cultivars are bred to encourage desirable qualities, such as the size and color of blooms or a longer flowering period. An amalgamation of wild species with cultivated variants can create a richer and more enduring plant display than either alone.

[Right] The planting at the Queen Elizabeth Olympic Park in London subtly mixes natives and non-natives and was designed by James Hitchmough, Nigel Dunnett, and Sarah Price. [Below] The famous High-Line planting in New York, designed by Piet Oudolf, mixes native and non-native species to dramatic effect.

[Top] In urban spaces, permeable surfaces, such as areas of planting, mitigate flash flooding. The Grey to Green scheme in Sheffield is the UK's largest retro-fit SuDS project (see pp.78–79) and the UK's largest inner-city "Green Street." Designed by Nigel Dunnett, Zac Tudor, and Robert Bray Associates, the scheme offers a calm refuge in an urban environment and a green space that encourages cycling and walking.
[Left] A sealed rainwater storage tank collects water from the adjacent roof.

GRAY WATER

Waste water from domestic settings—runoff from sinks, bathtubs, and showers—can be used to irrigate plants, as long as it has no fecal contamination. Test gray water on a sample area or on specific plants before using it for large-scale irrigation, and remember that certain cleaning products can have detrimental results, damaging soil or even killing plants.

WATER

ANALYZING YOUR SITE AND EXPLORING WATER FLOW AND STORAGE OPTIONS CAN INFORM YOU HOW TO USE THIS PRECIOUS RESOURCE MOST EFFICIENTLY.

To make the most of rainfall, whether it is scarce or plentiful, it is essential to understand how the water will move through and over the different surfaces of your garden, including roof structures, paving, soil, and plantings.

You can analyze this by paying attention to the way your site retains water: Are certain areas boggy? Does the ground feel soft underfoot? If so, this indicates poor drainage, which may need rectifying. On the other hand, cracked and degraded soil or dead plants can be signs that the site is prone to drought.

It's also worth considering whether any part of the site will be under water for a prolonged period of time—for example, a seasonal pond, swale, or stream. If so, what kind of plants and landscaping will be suitable for these areas?

Next, ask yourself how climate change will affect your garden. Will it be subject to increasingly heavy rainfall and freak weather events? Or will water be steadily scarcer, leading to periods of drought? You can assess this by referring to climate maps that predict the future climate in a given area (see p.42).

Once you have a clear idea of how water affects your plot, you can choose plants that will not only withstand the existing conditions, but will remedy them where needed. For example, in a plot that is too wet, consider plant species that will dry it out (see Chapter 5). In urban areas in particular, permeable surfaces, such as lawns or areas of planting, help prevent flash flooding.

WATER STORAGE

You can collect and store water using underground or surface tanks and containers, then use these reserves to irrigate planting through passive wicking systems, or filling your watering cans from the taps on a rain barrel. Storing rainwater in urban areas reduces water reaching mains sewers, which in turn works to prevent raw sewage being discharged into waterways and oceans. Rainwater will usually become contaminated with algae, which will block light from reaching plant leaves after about one week, but you can prolong its lifetime indefinitely by keeping it out of the light and away from animal and insect contact.

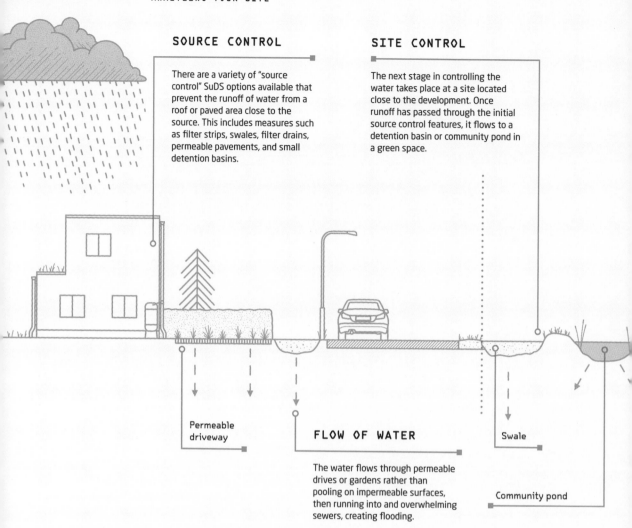

SOURCE CONTROL

There are a variety of "source control" SuDS options available that prevent the runoff of water from a roof or paved area close to the source. This includes measures such as filter strips, swales, filter drains, permeable pavements, and small detention basins.

SITE CONTROL

The next stage in controlling the water takes place at a site located close to the development. Once runoff has passed through the initial source control features, it flows to a detention basin or community pond in a green space.

Permeable driveway

FLOW OF WATER

The water flows through permeable drives or gardens rather than pooling on impermeable surfaces, then running into and overwhelming sewers, creating flooding.

Swale

Community pond

SUDS: SUSTAINABLE DRAINAGE STRATEGIES

SUSTAINABLE DRAINAGE SYSTEMS (REFERRED TO AS SUDS) RECREATE THE FORMATION OF WATER SYSTEMS THAT OCCUR NATURALLY. BY DOING THIS, THEY TEMPER THE NEGATIVE EFFECTS THAT MAN-MADE DEVELOPMENTS CAN HAVE ON THE FLOW OF WATER.

REGIONAL CONTROL

Large volumes of clean water from multiple developments flow to a regional control area. These regional controls feature in public spaces, such as wetlands and regional ponds.

Wetland

WATER SECURITY

In some parts of the world, it would already be considered shocking that drinking water is used to irrigate plants. By 2050, 5 billion people could be affected by water shortages, according to a UN report. Currently, more than 2 billion of the world's population do not have safe drinking water available in their homes, and it is predicted that by 2025, more than 50 percent of the world's population will live in places suffering from water stress. These figures have the potential to escalate if rates of climate change and the multiplying population follow or surpass predictions. The reduction in quality of water and decreasing levels of groundwater will restrict access to water for drinking and for growing food, which will lead to a host of political and socioeconomic difficulties. There will undoubtedly be societal damage unless urgent measures are taken to alleviate the stress on rivers, lakes, and other bodies of water.

SuDS imitate a flow of water similar to that of a nondeveloped site, expelling water into the surrounding environment in a regulated way. This minimizes the effect on the environment when it comes to collecting, storing, and cleaning water. It is also economically effective.

When thinking about sustainable drainage systems, it is imperative for gardeners and garden designers to consider the long-term impacts. For outdoor spaces on a large scale, this includes paying attention to the social needs of the area, as well as examining the volume of water that will drain away, considering the quality of the water, and the potential for it to be directed for use elsewhere. Reusing water could help maintain local green spaces. These systems address the issues of climate change and urbanization and set out a solution to water drainage problems (such as flooding) and the effects of pollution from runoff. SuDS can also be incorporated in gardens on a much smaller scale by including swales in the design (see p.136).

SUDS AND SEWAGE

Unfortunately, rivers and oceans are plagued by sewage and agricultural pollution. For example, in the UK in 2020, there were more than 400,000 discharges of untreated sewage into rivers and almost 5,500 discharges into UK coastal bathing waters. This is one of the several reasons why it is important to slow the flow of water through the landscape, and SuDS contribute to that.

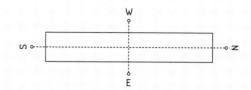

GARDEN AT 9A.M.

These three shadow plans show areas of shade in a garden in midsummer. This plan shows which areas of a will be in shade at 9a.m.

GARDEN AT 12 NOON

In the same garden at noon, there is only a minimal amount of shade, which is provided by the house and two trees.

GARDEN AT 4P.M.

At 4p.m., more of the garden falls into shade, but a large area in the middle and at the west-facing boundary remains exposed to the sun's glare.

SUN AND LIGHT

THE DIRECTION YOUR GARDEN FACES AND THE AMOUNT OF LIGHT AND SHADE IT EXPERIENCES ARE CRUCIAL TO THE CHOICES YOU MAKE ABOUT THE PLANTS YOU GROW.

The amount of sun that a garden receives is key to knowing what kind of conditions it will experience. Light is essential for plant growth and survival, and it can differ from one part of the site to another; for example, there will be a difference in light and heat levels on walls facing north, south, east, and west. Understanding the way that light moves through a space informs you how different areas will feel in terms of light, shade, and warmth and how plants will perform in each of them.

You can analyze the light conditions in your garden by simply observing how sunlight moves over it throughout the day year-round. Buildings, trees, fences, hedges, and structures can all block light, increasing shade, so factor this into your design decisions; bear in mind that future tall plantings in a garden can affect the light in neighboring spaces, too. If you would prefer a more detailed analysis, you can ask a professional garden designer to generate a 3D model of your plot using computer-aided design (CAD) software, showing the way light will fall on it.

SHADE LEVELS

The levels of shade need careful consideration when you are designing your garden, as plants need varying levels of sunlight. Planting sun-loving species in the shade, or vice versa, will mean they won't thrive and may even die. Sun and light also affect the way a garden will feel for people; shade-giving structures, or plants such as trees, climbers, and large shrubs, can offer respite in spaces exposed to the sun. Fast-growing species of climber, shrub, or tree can be cost-effective and environmentally friendly alternatives to building hard structures, such as covered pergolas.

TYPES OF SUN AND SHADE

Full sun More than six hours of direct sunlight each day during the summer.
Light shade The site is open to the sky, but an obstacle such as a group of trees screens it from direct sunlight.
Partial/semishade A plot that sees three to six hours of direct sun per day.
Dappled shade Light diffused through fairly open tree canopies.
Moderate shade A site receives sunlight for two or three hours per day.
Deep/heavy shade An area that receives less than two hours of sun per day, possibly shaded by trees or buildings.

WIND

HIGH WINDS CAN CAUSE DAMAGE IN A GARDEN, BUT WINDBREAKS AND DESIGNED FEATURES CAN CREATE SHELTER

Wind is an often overlooked factor in the garden, but it can have a serious impact on plants and our enjoyment of them. High winds can scorch leaves; damage plants; and, in some cases, kill them, if they are tender or in need of a sheltered site. You can analyze the amount of wind that affects your plot by looking for signs of damage or stress, such as stunted growth on existing plants.

To protect a site from prevailing winds, make use of windbreaks and shelterbelts. These are semipermeable masses of wind-resistant plants and trees that form a protective barrier. Designed elements, such as planters, walls, and screens, can also reduce wind speed and create shelter, resulting in a more comfortable space in which to enjoy your garden.

WHAT CAUSES WIND?

Wind can be a capricious element of our weather system, from a welcome gentle breeze on a sunny day to a ravaging force capable of ripping mature trees from their ancient standing. Although it's such a familiar presence, many of us aren't aware of what causes wind and dictates its behavior. The simple answer is temperature and, more specifically, the inconsistencies in temperature between different areas, such as land and sea. This creates contrasting atmospheric areas of low and high pressure, and when air moves between these areas, it results in a range of wind speeds and forces.

[Left] Windbreaks can be created using semipermeable masses of wind-resistant plants.
[Below] Winds can damage even well-established trees, from ripping branches off to felling an entire tree.

A hedge, a fence, or just a row of trees can create a windbreak in any garden. For a larger plot, a shelterbelt—a staggered planting of three or four rows of tall trees and shrubs, more than 15ft (4.5m) high—may be more suitable. All types must be semipermeable to keep them from being blown over or creating wind tunnels, when the wind is funneled along a valley between a line of trees or structures, potentially harming plants.

Trees, shrubs, and hedges are attractive and long-lasting, but they take a while to establish. If you're looking for a quick fix, you can buy screens and mix them with shrubs that will take longer to grow. Solid surfaces, including fences, won't be effective, as the wind will buffet up and over the top; instead, try woven fences of willow or hazel that will still allow some of the wind through. Ideally, a windbreak should filter 50–60 percent of the wind blowing toward it. Ensure that it is wider than the particular area that you're looking to protect; it will reduce the wind speed over a distance of 10 times its height.

WINDBREAKS AND SHELTERBELTS

WINDBREAKS AND SHELTERBELTS ARE SEMIPERMEABLE BARRIERS THAT REDUCE WIND SPEED AND PROVIDE SHELTER FOR PLANTS THAT STAND THROUGHOUT WINTER. THEY ALSO LESSEN THE RISK OF DAMAGE TO BUILDINGS AND PROVIDE SHELTER FOR WILDLIFE.

[Top] I designed these louvered timber screens to provide a windbreak for a productive area, while also bringing a beautiful element of design and zoning into the garden.

[Right] This artful woven screen by willow artisan Jay Davey flows through the garden. Its semipermeable surface reduces wind speed.

DROUGHT-TOLERANT PLANTING

In their experimental Mediterranean garden, Olivier and
Clara Filippi have developed drought-resilient planting
methods that are increasingly relevant worldwide.

OLIVIER FILIPPI is a pioneer of drought-tolerant planting, experimenting with plants in his nursery Le Jardin Sec in Southern France, and exploring resilient schemes as a necessary adaptation in the face of climate change and warmer, drier conditions.

"

WHAT KIND OF CHALLENGES ARE YOU FACING IN THE CHANGING MEDITERRANEAN CLIMATE?

Traditionally, many gardeners thought they had to choose mainly local species for a drought-tolerant garden, but there is a new view of this. If an invasive weed is the only plant able to survive in increasingly difficult conditions, that might be considered positive, because its interactions with birds and insects might lead to a hybrid range of native and non-native species. The garden becomes like an experimental lab of what could be the landscape of the future.

We have about 2,000 species, and some express their beauty through their drought-tolerance strategy—for example, *Phlomis* shed their leaves and produce new shoots covered in golden-brown hairs, giving a striking appearance. So drought is not a problem for design; it can mean more structure, volume, and texture in summer.

HOW IMPORTANT IS SUBSTRATE?

Very important, because we have summer drought and intense winter rainfall. Most of our plants are from eroded, rocky landscapes, so they would never face excessive water naturally. Their ability to survive such conditions is due to symbiosis [a mutually beneficial relationship] with bacteria or mycorrhiza, and these organisms need oxygen, which is not present in waterlogged soil.

HAVE YOU SEEN ANY ARCHETYPAL CHARACTERISTICS IN DROUGHT-TOLERANT PLANTS, AND HOW DO YOU SUCCESSFULLY ESTABLISH A DROUGHT-TOLERANT PLANTING SCHEME?

There are many and varied strategies available to plants in the wild, but grown in nursery conditions, drought-tolerant plants behave differently as their root systems are limited by pot size. We use anti-spin forestry pots to prevent roots from circling in the pots, which enables the plants to develop their proper double root system when they are planted in the garden. On the nursery we employ hardening techniques, watering and fertilizing as infrequently as possible, irrigating with salty brackish water so that the plants face an artificial drought, and inoculating with fungus for symbiosis.

When planting out, we never irrigate with a drip system as this encourages shallow rooting. During the first summer we water deeply once every three weeks, filling a watering basin around each plant to guide the roots deep down. The choice of species is key, but we must also prepare poor, well-oxygenated soil, plant in autumn before the rainfall, and select plants that have a similar volume of vegetation above ground and root system below.

AIR QUALITY

IS THE AIR IN YOUR GARDEN HEALTHY ENOUGH FOR PEOPLE AND PLANTS? IF NOT, THIS CAN BE IMPROVED WITH CONSIDERED PLANTING CHOICES.

Air quality will be affected by the location of your plot, whether it is near a busy road or airport, or in an urban environment that traps pollution. The quality can be assessed in simple terms by using your nose: Does the air smell fresh or polluted? Another method is to look at the amount of particulate matter captured on hard surfaces as black grime. The finer details of pollution can be assessed with air-quality monitors: small devices that analyze pollutants in the air and highlight potential risks to human health are now widely available.

Where gardens look on to busy roads, the types of plants you select can assist in cleaning the air by trapping particulates (see Chapter 5). In urban areas, parks and gardens act as green lungs, filtering and purifying air, removing gaseous and particulate pollutants. However, plants are the third line of defense, after reducing emissions and increasing the distance between us and the source of pollution.

DO GREEN WALLS FILTER AIR POLLUTION?

Pollution accumulates within enclosed street valleys, as it lacks an escape route. Based on a study conducted by Professor Rob MacKenzie of the University of Birmingham, UK, "green walls"—vertical swathes of grasses, ivy, and other plants—have the capacity to reduce pollution by more than 10 times the 1-2 percent originally thought.

Green walls in urban areas offer many benefits, including the capacity to reduce air pollution and provide a habitat for small animals and insects. I collaborated with Tapestry Vertical Gardens to design this backdrop wall for a residential dining area. The landscapers building the garden nicknamed it the RHS Television!

Singapore's air-quality initiatives include the "supertrees," which consist of 18 vertical gardens that generate solar power; collect rainwater; provide shade; and act as air venting ducts for nearby conservatories, using plants to filter the air.

[Top] Toads can help organically control slug and snail populations, as they predate on them. Including a water feature or pond in your garden will help attract amphibians, such as frogs and toads. [Right] A biodiverse planting scheme full of colorful perennials provides aesthetic interest as well as food sources for pollinators.

WILDLIFE

DOES WILDLIFE THRIVE IN YOUR GARDEN? LOOK FOR CLUES
TO DISCOVER WHICH ANIMALS AND INVERTEBRATES MIGHT BE
THERE AND HOW YOUR GARDENING STYLE CAN SUPPORT THEM.

Urbanization and increasing human populations mean that wildlife habitats are disappearing at an alarming rate. We are in the midst of a biodiversity crisis, with many species declining rapidly across the globe. Designing our garden spaces in a way that means we can share them with wildlife is not difficult—it just takes a little forethought and potentially a shift in our expectations of what makes a garden beautiful and functional.

To discover the wildlife in your garden, look for tracks, feces, damage to plants (such as nibbled leaves and scraped bark), and holes in structures or the ground. Then consider the potential for wildlife: Are you near a forest, a coast, or a road? What forms of wildlife are you likely to find in your area and how can you attract those species to your own space? Certain species, such as rabbits, deer, and some insects, can cause significant damage, but there are nondestructive methods that keep them out, such as fencing, caging, and covering, or organic and biological controls.

> Designing our garden spaces in a way that means we can share them with wildlife is not difficult—it just takes a little forethought and potentially a shift in our expectations of what makes a garden beautiful and functional.

INSECTS

Insects—often overlooked and underappreciated—are a key part of the food chain, providing sustenance for birds and mammals. Pollinating insects are key to global food security, as we rely on them for the pollination of vital crops. Their decline will cause immeasurable problems for humans and lead to global food shortages, but gardeners can go some way toward offsetting the damage that is caused by pesticides.

Creating a garden that functions as an ecosystem and supports wildlife all the way up the food chain is key to climate resilience. Think creatively—for example, add a pond to attract toads and frogs that eat slugs, and put bird feeders next to plants that suffer from caterpillar damage. This can create a balanced, self-sustaining garden that doesn't need constant—and potentially harmful—human intervention.

CHAPTER FOUR

CLIMATE RESILIENT GARDEN DESIGN

RESILIENT GARDEN DESIGN

THIS CHAPTER DEMONSTRATES HOW SOME OF THE IDEAS THAT HAVE BEEN DISCUSSED IN THE BOOK SO FAR CAN BE PUT INTO PRACTICE IN EVEN A RELATIVELY SMALL SPACE THAT IS TYPICAL OF MANY URBAN GARDENS.

Do we need to heavily control our gardens, or is a light touch more sustainable? The answer is that by aiming for a looser, more "wild" aesthetic, we can reduce the need for intervention. Abandoning the idea that "neatness" is attainable or even desirable in a garden or landscape allows us to aim instead for a resilient and wildlife-friendly area that is created with sustainable materials. By using ecological design principles, we can encourage plenty of biodiversity in a garden that flourishes naturally instead of one that needs constant human intervention to keep it looking attractive.

VIRTUAL REALITY

We have worked with graphic visualization company AVA to create a virtual front and rear garden inspired by the principles discussed in this book. The images of the resilient garden throughout the book are computer generated. To enrich the experience of understanding the garden design, you can explore it via the QR code here, using a smartphone, tablet, computer, or VR headset.

WWW.DK.COM/RESILIENT-GARDEN

A timber boardwalk floats through the
resilient garden, crossing a water feature
and passing through a forest garden planting
full of edible delights.

FRONT GARDEN
SITE ANALYSIS

The original site is an end-of-terrace house in a built-up urban environment, with a busy road running adjacent to the property (to the right of this image). Not only is the front garden space dull, it is not environmentally friendly, and nor does it provide much benefit to wildlife or to those living in the house.

DEGRADED SOIL

The soil is poor quality—dry, degraded, and full of rubble. Hard landscaping has created a harsh, sterile environment.

HARD SURFACES AND COOLING PLANTS

Heat islands in cities are caused partly by the lack of natural landscapes and the materials used in urban developments. Traditional fabricated materials—those used for roofing, pavements, roads, and vehicles—absorb and release more heat from the sun's rays than vegetation does. These solid, hard, dark surfaces are less efficient at deflecting solar energy, with the result that there is less shade and less moisture in the air, causing the temperature to rise. In urban settings, heat builds and is stored over the course of the day; as the sun sets and the temperature drops, the heat is then radiated out into the environment.

Areas of vegetation and water are naturally effective at cooling the air and keeping temperatures down. Trees offer shade; plant leaves exude moisture; and rivers and ponds evaporate surface water, cooling the atmosphere with water vapor.

POOR PLANT CHOICES

The box hedge (*Buxus sempervirens*) is in poor condition. Box is susceptible to pests and diseases, in particular box-moth caterpillar and box blight. It needs time-consuming maintenance and often harmful chemical treatments to keep it looking pristine.

EXPOSED PLOT

The front garden is exposed and suffers from drying winds. Air quality in the space is poor: a busy road runs to the east and there is no barrier between the garden and the road, so the traffic is in full view and there is no protection from air and noise pollution. Excessive hard landscaping has created a harsh and sterile environment.

HOSTILE HABITATS

The garden has very few signs of wildlife, apart from the caterpillars that have been eating the box hedge. No provision has been made for any habitats, nor has the planting been designed to support biodiversity and encourage wildlife.

HEAT TRAP

The south-facing aspect of the garden and lack of planting means this space is very hot. It offers no shading for the house nor to cool the space.

IMPERMEABLE SURFACE

Water runs over the impermeable paving right into the sanitary sewers, wasting a valuable resource and contributing to flooding when rainfall is excessive.

FRONT GARDEN RESILIENT DESIGN

The front garden design offers a solution that is focused on improving the local environment, benefiting wildlife, and improving the well-being of those using the garden.

RECLAIMED MATERIALS
pp.148–151

Waste materials have been used in the paving—a terrazzolike material using site rubble as an aggregate. This shows how trash can be made into treasure if it is treated and processed in creative ways (see pp.224–225).

BIODIVERSE HABITATS
pp.140–143

A biodiverse mix of plants for pollinators provides food for insects, drawing them to the garden. Several wildlife habitat panels have also been built in the garden, providing shelter for insects and other invertebrates.

MINERAL MULCH
pp.128-129

The recycled aggregate gravel acts as a mineral mulch while bringing a Mediterranean feel to the garden. The gravel areas and channels between paving slabs have been populated with colorful, drought-tolerant, scented plants that are able to deal with the polluted site, poor soil, and hot conditions. Rugged and tough species, such as thyme, spill out onto the drive.

PROTECTIVE BOUNDARIES
pp.138-139

Hedges and trees cool the air, reduce the impact of the wind, and provide food and shelter for wildlife. Dense hedges provide a barrier from the busy road, with species that have been selected for their ability to capture pollutants (see pp.170-171).

PASSIVE IRRIGATION
pp.134-135

The paving has been replaced by permeable recycled aggregate gravel. A rainwater harvesting system stops surface water from running off the drive into sewer drains, and this passively irrigates the plants.

REAR GARDEN SITE ANALYSIS

The original rear garden is as dull as the front garden. The garden offers little benefit to wildlife, with limited biodiversity, except for a thriving rowan tree (*Sorbus aucuparia*). Valuable water is wasted, as there is no means of storing rainwater.

WASTED WATER

Water that falls on the roof of the garden office is diverted into the strip of soil behind the building, wasting a resource on an area of the garden in which very little will grow.

DULL VIEW

The view from the garden office is of the dead ash tree, which is depressing. The glazed façade faces west, with little cover from the sun now that the tree has no foliage, which creates a hot internal environment.

STARK BOUNDARIES

The boundaries are softwood timber fences in good condition. They offer some shelter to the site, so the rear garden does not suffer from the same drying winds as the front. However, nothing is growing on them, so they feel stark and imposing, boxing in the space instead of creating a feeling of sanctuary.

LACK OF BIODIVERSITY

The rear garden is a little more wildlife-friendly than the front but lacks biodiversity in the planting; there are few flowering plants for pollinating insects to visit.

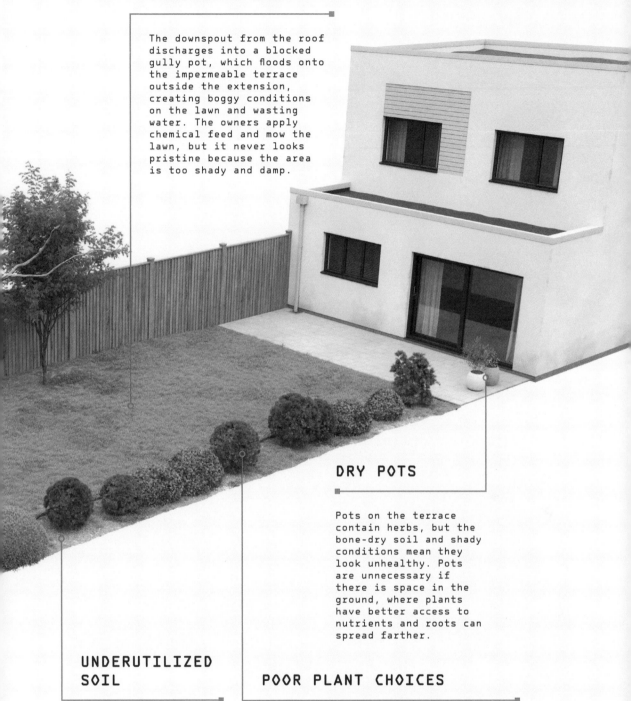

UNHEALTHY LAWN

The downspout from the roof discharges into a blocked gully pot, which floods onto the impermeable terrace outside the extension, creating boggy conditions on the lawn and wasting water. The owners apply chemical feed and mow the lawn, but it never looks pristine because the area is too shady and damp.

DRY POTS

Pots on the terrace contain herbs, but the bone-dry soil and shady conditions mean they look unhealthy. Pots are unnecessary if there is space in the ground, where plants have better access to nutrients and roots can spread farther.

UNDERUTILIZED SOIL

The soil is not of bad quality; a soil test shows it to be a pH-neutral natural loam. This is a good general-purpose soil that could be improved by adding organic matter. Some builders' rubble exists at the back, around the tree.

POOR PLANT CHOICES

The planting to the side of the lawn is dull and mainly evergreen—a mix of clipped topiary balls and drab shrubs. At the rear, a large ash tree (*Fraxinus excelsior*) has succumbed to ash dieback.

REAR GARDEN RESILIENT DESIGN

The rear garden has been transformed into a biodiverse area full of life, texture, color, and interest, with multiple new trees and an understory planting beneficial to local wildlife, and attractive to those using the garden.

FOOD FOREST
pp.114-115

The lawn is gone; it was in poor condition and offered little visual or wildlife benefit. The planting follows a "food forest" concept (see p.53), where edible plants coexist with ornamental species in a layered understory. This kind of planting uses species known as "edimentals"(see pp.180-197 for a list of edimental plants).

RECLAIMED MATERIALS
pp.148-151

A reclaimed timber boardwalk "floats" over the garden, creating a dynamic and immersive walkway. Plants and wildlife are able to occupy space beneath it, lowering the impact of the hardscape. It could be removed with little damage to the garden, and the environmental impact of its disposal would be minimal, as timber is a biodegradable material.

COMPOST AREA
pp.122-125

A compost area allows green garden waste to be utilized. Compost can be applied to the planting, enriching the soil and creating a healthy and circular ecosystem.

CONNECTING WITH NATURE
pp.154-155

The layout brings planting close to the house. From inside, a framed view of a tree increases the connection with nature even when the inhabitants are indoors.

BIODIVERSE HABITATS
pp.140-143

Five new multistemmed trees evoke a woodland edge atmosphere and associate with the rowan, which has been pruned to allow light to the plants beneath it. As well as providing protection from sun and wind, the trees are a mix of fruiting and flowering species that offer food for humans, animals, and insects.

RECLAIMED MATERIALS
pp.148-151

The use of hard paving has been minimized to increase permeability; paved areas have been limited to providing hard standing for the dining table and access to the doors into the house. Channels for planting and gravel break up the hard surface, making it permeable and less hard and sterile than the previous mortar-jointed paving. The paving is the same recycled terrazzo that is used at the front.

WILDLIFE POND
pp.144-145

The garden includes a pond that fills with rainwater runoff from the roof during the wetter seasons, which provides a habitat for wildlife and encourages beneficial predators into the garden, such as toads and frogs.

GREEN ROOF
pp.108-109

A green roof has been laid on the roof of both the house and the rear extension, providing insulating properties, added wildlife benefit, and reducing storm-water runoff.

REWILDED AREA
pp.116-117

The main area of the garden has essentially been rewilded. This informal design approach embraces a wild aesthetic and provides vital habitats for wildlife, including insect species that are in decline due in large part to habitat loss. The boundaries and the garden office have been covered in climbing plants and wildlife habitat panels.

SUDS PLANTER
pp.136-137

The downspout from the roof now discharges into a SuDS planter, with plants that tolerate both dry conditions and occasional waterlogging. In heavy rainfall, the water discharges into a swale, which collects runoff water from the roof of the house and hard surfaces in the garden, and fills the wildlife pond.

ORGANIC MULCH
pp.126-127

All of the planted areas in the resilient garden design have been mulched. A protective layer of material covers the soil, emulating natural landscapes where bare earth is rarely found.

HUGELKULTUR MOUNDS

pp.146-147

Wood from the dead ash tree and other organic waste, such as the removed turf, has been piled into a hugel mound. These contoured mounds provide interesting landscape features as well as nutrients and moisture for plants.

MUSHROOM LOGS

pp.152-153

The dead ash tree has been reused in multiple ways, including as informal seats, both sawn and natural, and as logs to grow mushrooms.

RAINWATER HARVESTING

pp.132-133

A SuDS rain barrel planter has been added to capture water from the roof of the garden office. This can be used to water the garden by hand when needed.

BIODIVERSE ROOF

pp.110-111

The garden office now has a biodiverse roof that is a mix of waste materials, including dead wood and crushed concrete from the build. It has been seeded with native wildflowers and designed to provide visual impact and habitats for insects.

SIDE-BY-SIDE COMPARISON

The plan views of the original and resilient garden show a stark comparison. There are many changes we can make to improve the sustainability and resilience of our gardens.

ORIGINAL FRONT GARDEN

This is a stark and sterile space with abundant hard landscaping and very little room for planting. Hot and south-facing, it feels stark, exposed, and lacking in life and atmosphere.

RESILIENT FRONT GARDEN

The parking space is retained, but the hard paving is replaced with permeable gravel. New trees and gravel-garden planting cool the space and provide atmosphere and interest as well as food and habitat for visiting wildlife.

ORIGINAL REAR GARDEN

A large area of lawn and wide
expanses of paving mean the garden
is very open and lacking in interest.
Planting is limited and struggling,
while a dead tree offers a depressing
view from the garden studio.

RESILIENT REAR GARDEN

The lawn and paving have been replaced
by landscape features that sustain
wildlife. The planting creates a dynamic
space offering visual interest and
forageable treats. Rainwater is slowed
and collected for sustainable use.

GREEN ROOF

A GREEN ROOF CONSISTS OF A LAYER OF PLANTING AND GROWING MEDIUM (SUBSTRATE) SET OVER A WATERPROOF MEMBRANE ON EITHER A FLAT OR PITCHED ROOF. PREGROWN GREEN ROOF SYSTEMS ARE AVAILABLE AND GENERALLY EASY TO INSTALL.

A green roof can be considered for a pitched roof, but if your roof has a slope more severe than 9.5 degrees, take extra measures to secure the substrate and consider a solution for water retention, because water will run off the steeper pitch. Have your roof checked by a structural engineer first to make sure it can take the added weight, and consult local planning laws. Green roofs can generally be placed into three categories: extensive, intensive, and semi-intensive.

EXTENSIVE

This type of roof (see right) has a shallow growing substrate, usually less than 6in (150mm). It weighs only moderately on the roof and has a limited range of plants, for example, a mix of sedum species. It is usually inaccessible and low maintenance, able to thrive with minimal watering or none at all in wet climates or with suitable planting mixes.

INTENSIVE

With a deeper substrate, up to 3¼ft (1m) or more, intensive green roofs make a heavier load on the structure. They can bear a wider variety of plants and even small trees and will usually require maintenance and frequent watering. They often take the form of roof gardens.

SEMI-INTENSIVE

A semi-intensive roof shares qualities with both extensive and intensive green roofs. The depth of the substrate, and therefore the plants you are able to include, is dependent on the structure and integrity of the roof, the level of annual rainfall, and any water harvesting capacity such as passive irrigation (see pp.134–135) included in the design.

On the biodiverse roof of the garden office,
a substrate of crushed construction waste
has been allowed to self-seed with local
species blown in by the wind or deposited
by animals. Dead wood provides habitat.

BIODIVERSE ROOF

THE ROOF OF THE GARDEN OFFICE HAS BEEN TRANSFORMED INTO A BIODIVERSE ROOF. BOTH BROWN AND BIODIVERSE ROOFS ARE AN EFFECTIVE WAY TO RECREATE THE UNCULTIVATED URBAN AREAS FOUND AT GROUND LEVEL, WITH PLANTS OF THE SAME KIND ABLE TO POPULATE THE ROOF SPACE.

On a biodiverse roof, the substrate medium is seeded or planted at the time of construction. Such roofs are considered by many urban planning bodies to be a natural extension of the landscape that provides further habitats for insect life and a variety of plant species.

An alternative to a biodiverse roof is a brown roof. Here, the substrate medium is left to self-seed via airborne dispersal and other natural means, such as bird droppings. However, biodiverse roofs achieve a more instant and designed impact as a result of purposeful planting and seeding.

INSTALLATION

Brown and biodiverse roofs typically do not require any irrigation and are naturally low maintenance. The depth of the substrate tends to be up to 6in (150mm), with a medium weight pressure, in general no more than 2½ cwt per 1¼ sq yd (120kg per m²). This can support stones, rocks, and decaying timber, which attracts insects and other wildlife. Brown and biodiverse roofs can also insulate a building, helping regulate the temperature as well as improving acoustics.

You can incorporate sustainable materials by using recycled aggregate in the substrate, such as construction waste material and rubble that has been washed—but, when using waste from a building site, make sure that the material does not contain contaminated matter or sharp fragments that might damage the waterproof membrane below. Once it has become established, a brown roof will mature into a green roof as wind-borne seeds settle and develop into colonies of plants.

BIODIVERSE HABITATS

John has experimented with substrates ranging from rubble and sand to chalk and crushed ceramics, yielding exciting results for biodiversity in the garden.

JOHN LITTLE is a living roof and brownfield gardening expert and the founder of the Grass Roof Company. He plants inspiring biodiverse habitats, including his own garden, where he experiments with an array of waste materials for habitat provision and as a growing medium for resilient plants.

66

WHY ARE BROWNFIELD LANDSCAPES SO INSPIRING TO YOU?

The combination of substrates and materials creates places for biodiversity to thrive, and their complexity makes them great for wildlife. They are harsh environments, so nettles, brambles, and docks have less chance to establish, and the species that like less competition, such as wildflowers that grow on poor or chalky soils, can thrive. If we can be inspired by brownfield sites and bring some of this chaos into our gardens using waste materials destined for landfills, so much the better.

HOW IMPORTANT DO YOU THINK IT IS THAT WE INCLUDE HABITAT IN OUR LANDSCAPES AND GARDENS?

The Great Dixter Biodiversity Audit of 2017–2019, from a garden in Sussex, showed that a garden is not just a mass of plants as a food source for pollinators—it's also about buildings, dry-stone walls, dead wood, and compost heaps, which are great for biodiversity. In the yard where we build our products, thousands of invertebrates live in the piles of waste materials that we generate, which encourages biodiversity. You can place waste materials in your garden in an ordered fashion to improve its biodiversity by creating much-needed habitat and shelter.

HOW DO YOU DESIGN A RESILIENT GREEN OR BROWN ROOF THAT WILL STAND THE TEST OF TIME?

First, you must ensure the roof will take the added weight. As you would on the ground, integrate a mix of materials— structural elements such as log piles are key to creating a roof that is beneficial for biodiversity. A harsh substrate is important to stop competition and slow succession—you don't want a rich and fertile environment, as it won't survive the conditions of the rooftop setting, where the plants need to be resilient.

113

Lawns often contain limited or monoculture plant species, so they have low biodiversity and negligible wildlife value. Many people see a lawn as an essential element for children to play on, but alternative types of gardens offer a sensory treasure trove where children can explore and really engage with the natural environment. Lawns can be replaced with many different types of planting to create a richer, more atmospheric, and biodiverse environment.

EDIMENTAL PLANTING

A fusion of the words "ornamental" and "edible," often used to describe plants, "edimental" is a term coined to describe those that provide both of these qualities. Edimentals are a great way to increase the productivity of a garden while also keeping it looking aesthetically pleasing. Some edimentals have leaves and shoots that can be eaten, while others have edible flowers, roots, or tubers—but check before consuming, as only certain parts of the plant may be edible. Always ensure that you know what is safe to eat, because certain plants and fungi are poisonous and even deadly.

GREEN CARPETS

It is not only grass that can tolerate foot traffic. Many plants are low-growing and hug the ground to form green carpets, including creeping thyme (*Thymus praecox*) and mind-your-own-business (*Soleirolia soleirolii*). A mixture of ground-covering plants requires less maintenance than a single-species carpet and also provides more resilience and biodiversity.

SPECIES-RICH LAWNS

A grass lawn will try to revert to a mixed grassland if it is not regularly mowed and weeded. A lawn richer in species is easier to maintain and sustain than a single-species monoculture. Allowing some dandelions, clover, and other wild flowering species into your lawn provides food for popular pollinators such as bees and butterflies.

FOOD FOREST

LUSH GREEN LAWNS USUALLY REQUIRE HUGE AMOUNTS OF FERTILIZER, WATER, AND MAINTENANCE TO KEEP THE DESIRED GREEN AESTHETIC YEAR-ROUND, SO CONSIDER A FOOD FOREST FULL OF VARIED EDIMENTAL PLANTS INSTEAD.

LAYERS OF THE FOOD FOREST

The planting of the food forest, or forest garden, takes inspiration from the layers found in a natural woodland:
1 Canopy: The highest layer of trees, spaced to allow light to permeate through to the lower layers.
2 Small trees: Beneath the canopy of taller trees.
3 Shrubs: Tolerant of partial shade.
4 Herbaceous perennials: Die back in winter and return in the spring, opening up space for fall- and spring-flowering bulbs.
5 Ground cover: Creeping and carpeting plants that suppress weeds and cover and protect the soil.
6 Climbers: Scrambling upward toward light, they generally require trees or structures for support.
7 The soil, roots, and fungi.

[Left] Large swathes of monoculture lawn are high maintenance and of low value to wildlife. [Below] Replacing a lawn with a biodiverse mix of plants creates a haven for wildlife as well as an uplifting and immersive aesthetic display.

[Right] The contrast of before and after is quite stark when seen side by side; the flat lawn and drab shrubs look dull and lifeless in contrast to the abundant and biodiverse planting.
[Below] Planting in a randomized matrix rather than formal blocks will give a natural and wild feel. Some "weeds" can remain if they are not invasive and provide benefit, such as food for pollinators or nitrogen-fixing properties.

REWILDED AREA

REWILDING IS DEFINED AS "RESTORATION OF ECOSYSTEMS TO THE POINT WHERE NATURE IS ALLOWED TO TAKE CARE OF ITSELF." THIS MEANS REINSTATING NATURAL PROCESSES AND REINTRODUCING SPECIES THAT HAVE DECLINED OR DISAPPEARED, THEN ALLOWING THEM TO SHAPE THE LANDSCAPE AND HABITATS.

CULTIVATED WILD

Rewilding encourages people to reconnect with nature, and this can be implemented even in a small garden. The resilient garden aims to be a "cultivated wild"—an augmented version of a natural landscape. The design achieves this with loose and informal planting, including a biodiverse mix of plants in naturalistic groupings; habitats added to encourage predators into the garden to feed on pests, including bird feeders, insect habitats, and a wildlife pond; an absence of harmful chemicals for fertilizers, sterilizing, or pest and weed control; and garden waste composted on site, with the compost utilized to improve the soils for growing.

The wild aesthetic should be included wherever possible. Allowing a less visible area of the garden to go wild—such as the boundaries, where the garden bleeds into the wider landscape—could be a good compromise to gain the benefits without losing a "tidy" aesthetic in more visible areas.

WILD NATURE IN THE GARDEN

One way of storing carbon in your soil is to cover it with plants. Incorporating organic matter into your soil beforehand helps lock in carbon and adds nutrients to the soil to help plants flourish. Growing deep-rooting plants will then capture carbon through photosynthesis and feed it to the soil. In simple terms, the more plants the better.

HOW PLANTS ABSORB CARBON DIOXIDE

In the same way that humans need oxygen to survive, plants take up carbon dioxide, and by using photosynthesis, they transform it into glucose, a vital energy source the plant needs to grow. They also release oxygen as a byproduct of photosynthesis. By increasing the number of plants and reducing hard landscaping, you can make your garden more effective at absorbing carbon, acting as a living, breathing lung; expelling oxygen; and purifying the air. This is a great excuse for any green-fingered enthusiast to indulge in more plants.

PROTECTING YOUR SOIL

Healthy soil acts as a carbon sink by drawing carbon into it. Plants capture carbon dioxide in their leaves through photosynthesis, then pump the carbon underground through their roots. Simply leaving soil undisturbed will allow it to store the carbon.

THE STATE OF THE SOIL

Soil degradation is a global problem, affecting a third of the world's arable soils. While soil takes thousands of years to form, an area the size of 30 soccer fields is destroyed worldwide every minute through erosion, which means we lose fertile soil for growing food, and the carbon stored within it is released. However, by gardening sustainably, composting, mulching, protecting, and organically improving soils in our own plots, we gardeners can help.

NO-DIG GARDENING

Disturbing the soil as little as possible prevents the soil structure from being damaged and stops carbon from being released into the atmosphere. British organic gardener Charles Dowding is a pioneer of the no-dig approach. The main benefits of it are:

- When left undisturbed, soil has less need to recover, so it grows fewer weeds.
- Undisturbed soil is full of organisms and microbes that help plants find the nutrients and moisture they need. Eating vegetables grown in this type of soil is beneficial to your own health by improving your gut microbiome.

ATMOSPHERIC CARBON DIOXIDE

Plants absorb carbon dioxide from the atmosphere and turn it into oxygen. Rising levels of carbon dioxide in the atmosphere increase plant photosynthesis, known as the carbon fertilization effect.

SUGARS

Plants use the energy of the sun to turn water and carbon dioxide into glucose, which is then used by the plants for energy and to make other substances, such as cellulose and starch.

BACTERIA

Sugars from plant roots feed bacteria colonies. Bacteria break down soil particles into nutrients for plants and convert energy into humus—the organic component of soil, which lasts for decades as soil carbon.

MYCORRHIZAL FUNGI

These beneficial fungal strands connected to plant roots take sugar from the plant and in exchange give the plant moisture and nutrients from the soil.

119

WILDING URBAN SPACES

Thomas founded Phyto Studio with Melissa Rainer and
Claudia West to create artistic, technically driven design
solutions for resilient and beautiful planting schemes.

THOMAS RAINER is a landscape architect and a leading voice in ecological landscape design. A specialist in using pioneering planting concepts to design ecologically functional landscapes, he is influenced by wild landscapes in his designs for planting schemes that thrive in the urban environment.

HOW DO YOU DEFINE A RESILIENT PLANTING SCHEME?

Resilient planting means an alignment of site conditions, plant palette, and human management. For a new site, we try to understand what its natural ecological trajectory would be: Which invasive species are in the seed bank or likely to migrate in? Which stresses (drought, disturbance, herbivory) will shape its future?

Next, we select plants that can survive with minimal input. If drought and low-productivity soils are the driving factors, can we build a plant palette with stress-tolerating species? If we have a rain garden with excess moisture and fertility, can we use well-behaved competitors to absorb excess nutrients and water?

Finally, we consider the management of a scheme. Will it be high or low maintenance? Will it be cut back with a mower or trimmer? Then the palette is simplified to species that are suited to that management regime. Next, we eliminate those that are prone to dominate.

HOW IMPORTANT IS SOIL OR SUBSTRATE IN A SCHEME?

Our entire palette is based on specific soil conditions. On urban sites, we may create stressful soils so we can use short, floriferous planting schemes that thrive in such conditions. Shorter plantings often require low-fertility soils; highly productive soils often produce competitive vegetation that flops. Using gravel or coarse sand in the top 6–8in (15–20cm) can help reduce fertility and weed growth.

HOW DO YOU APPROACH PLANTING DESIGN FOR A SPECIFIC SITE?

We use naturally occurring plant communities so the entire community will be stable over time. The dynamic qualities of species should balance each other; for example, if some taller species are winter-dormant, the ground layer beneath will be winter-green. If one species blooms in early summer, another will bloom in midsummer. By selecting plants with distinct shapes and behaviors, we can cover the soil with vegetation to protect it.

COMPOSTING IN A SMALL SPACE

In any garden, even a small one, composting is beneficial. If you are short on space, consider worm composting or an off-the-shelf compost bin, many of which are designed to heat the compost to high temperatures, speeding up the composting process and making it more efficient. Fairly new to the market are electric composters that function like kitchen appliances and turn food waste into usable compost in a matter of hours. They can provide a handy way to deal with food and kitchen waste, leaving the outdoor heap or bin for composting garden waste only.

COMPOSTING TIPS

The microorganisms (bacteria and fungi) that transform waste material into compost work most effectively when they are kept at consistent levels of temperature and moisture, so make use of a shady corner of the garden, perhaps behind a shed or somewhere else out of sight. A bin placed on an earth base provides easy drainage and allows access to the organisms in the soil. If your bin is on a hard surface, you can add a layer of garden soil to the compost bin to introduce those organisms.

Most home compost bins on the market should produce usable compost, provided they keep out most of the rain, let in air, permit drainage, and maintain some warmth, though small bins (less than 1¼cu yd/1cu m) are less effective than larger ones. As bins reserve heat and moisture, they speed up the composting process, but a traditional open heap in the garden will compost down with time.

PLANT NUTRIENTS

To mature and flourish, all plants need a blend of different nutrients, though the quantities of these depend on the species of plant and its stage of growth. Plants extract carbon, oxygen, and hydrogen from the air; the three primary nutrients they derive from the soil are nitrogen, phosphorus, and potassium, with magnesium, calcium, and sulfur in lesser quantities. In areas where these nutrients are absent, or if you want your plants to produce maximum flowers and fruit, you can add nutrients with natural fertilizers, including homemade compost.

COMPOST AREA

COMPOSTING YOUR KITCHEN AND GARDEN WASTE AT HOME IS ENVIRONMENTALLY FRIENDLY AND HAS THE ADDED BENEFIT OF PROVIDING MATERIAL THAT CAN IMPROVE YOUR SOIL. WHILE LOCAL AUTHORITIES OFTEN PROVIDE COLLECTIONS FOR GREEN WASTE, COMPOSTING AT HOME HAS A LOWER CARBON FOOTPRINT.

A timber composting bin is unobtrusive and fits in with
the natural aesthetic of the garden. Tucked away in a
shady corner, a bin deals with garden waste, reduces the
carbon footprint associated with transporting it off site,
and saves money and waste associated with store-bought
bagged compost.

02

GREEN MATERIALS

Aim for between 25 and 50 percent soft green materials (grass clippings, annual weeds, uncooked fruit and vegetable kitchen waste) to feed the microorganisms. Do not have one material dominating the heap, especially grass clippings, as these can become a slimy mess.

01

BROWN MATERIALS

The remainder of the heap should be brown woody material, such as prunings, wood chippings, paper, cardboard, straw, dead leaves, and plant stems.

01

Examples of brown compost materials: [1] Dead leaves **[2]** Uncoated cardboard and paper **[3]** Wood ash

Examples of green compost materials:
[1] Uncooked plant-based food waste [2] Garden prunings [3] Grass clippings from mowing the lawn

TURNING THE HEAP

Air is essential for composting to happen—if the heap becomes too condensed or waterlogged, the composting process slows down. Turning the heap incorporates air, and neglecting to do this is probably the main reason why composting might not work. Ideally, turn it about once a month. This also gives you an opportunity to gauge the moisture level in the heap—be especially vigilant during drier months.

WHEN IS THE COMPOST READY?

Garden compost is usually ready to use in six months to two years, depending on the amount of heat and moisture it receives. Ripe compost should have a dark brown hue and smell like a damp forest floor, with a texture resembling soil. There will probably be some material that has not rotted down sufficiently, but that can be incorporated into the next heap to be recomposted.

TROUBLESHOOTING

- **Sodden, slimy, smelly compost** This is usually a result of too much moisture, perhaps caused by poor drainage and not enough air. Shield the heap with a cover and add extra brown waste.
- **Dry and fibrous compost that hasn't rotted** This is caused by the heap being too dry, with too much brown material. Add more green waste, or fresh manure (1 bucket per 6in/15cm layer of compost).
- **Flies** A well-managed compost heap should not attract flies, but if they become a problem, cover any kitchen waste with a layer of garden waste. Check that there isn't too much moisture in the heap, restricting the air.

ORGANIC MULCH

MULCH IS THE MATERIAL LAID OVER THE SURFACE OF BARE SOIL OR ON TOP OF COMPOST IN CONTAINERS. ALL OF THE PLANTED AREAS IN THE RESILIENT GARDEN DESIGN ARE MULCHED. AN ORGANIC MULCH IS GENERALLY LAID IN A LAYER OF AT LEAST 2IN (5CM) THICK DURING LATE FALL TO LATE WINTER.

Mulches emulate natural landscapes, where soil is rarely found without some kind of organic or inorganic covering, such as leaf mold in a forest or scree on a mountainside. In the garden, mulching is beneficial in many different ways. It enhances the quality of the soil and promotes plant growth by introducing extra nutrients while encouraging advantageous organisms and deterring those that can damage plants, such as slugs and snails. It helps the soil retain moisture and suppress weeds, saving time and resources used on watering and weeding. Finally, it can warm the ground in spring while keeping it moist and cool in the dry months of summer, protecting plant roots from high temperatures, and, in the winter, shielding them from frost and cold.

BIODEGRADABLE MATERIAL

Organic mulches can consist of any biodegradable material, which means anything that doesn't remain in the environment indefinitely and can be broken down by fungi, bacteria, and microorganisms. Materials commonly used include garden compost, cardboard, well-rotted farmyard manure, composted bark, wood chips, seaweed, straw, and used hops (but note that hops are toxic and potentially lethal to dogs and, less often, to cats).

Ideally, material described as biodegradable should not take long to break down and should not leave anything behind that is detrimental to the environment—but some biodegradable materials such as bioplastics, can need specialized processes in order to break down, which is not ideal for a garden setting, so their use as a mulch should be avoided. As the mulch decays into the soil, the top layers will need replacing periodically.

POTENTIAL PROBLEMS

Applied correctly, mulches are reliably useful, but if you mulch too deep, close to the stems of trees or shrubs, the stem can weaken, exposing the plant to disease.

If you are mulching to discourage weeds and retain moisture, the depth of the mulch is more important than the choice of material. A shallow layer of mulch will fail to minimize evaporation from the surface of the soil and regulate the temperature, and it will allow weeds access to sunlight, which will encourage their growth.

A garden compost that has not been effectively rotted down can introduce weeds, pests, and diseases. With wood chips, there is a potential risk of honey fungus exposure if the chips are infected. If the fungus is already present in the garden, using a clean commercial mulch won't increase risk to other plants. However, if you chip your own wood, ensure you choose only material that is free of honey fungus, as even small bits of contaminated wood can infect plants. Bark chips are thought to be lower risk than wood-chip mulch.

An organic mulch—such as composted bark, leaf mold, or garden compost—is a great way to protect soil from erosion, lock in moisture, suppress weeds, and add nutrients.

Drought-resilient perennials, grasses, and shrubs are flourishing here in a recycled aggregate mulch, creating a Mediterranean feel to the garden. Many of these plants grow in stony and rocky landscapes, so the mulch mimics their natural environment and helps protect the plants from winter wet, which is very important for their long-term health.

MINERAL MULCH

NONBIODEGRADABLE MATERIALS CAN ALSO BE USED AS EFFECTIVE MULCHES. SLATE, SHINGLE, PEBBLES, GRAVEL, AND STONE CHIPPINGS ARE ALL EXAMPLES OF NONBIODEGRADABLE MULCH. IN THE RESILIENT GARDEN DESIGN, THE GRAVEL GARDEN USES RECYCLED AGGREGATE AS A MINERAL MULCH.

Just like biodegradable mulches, nonbiodegradable mulches discourage weeds by masking the sunlight needed for their seeds to germinate and retain moisture by providing a barrier, thus minimizing water evaporation from the soil. However, they do not enhance the structure or fertility of the soil.

The color of the mulch can make a difference: dark mulches, such as slate, will absorb heat and help keep the soil warm, whereas light-colored gravel will keep roots cool in an area of intense sun exposure by reflecting the heat of the sun's rays. A depth of 4in (10cm) will protect the soil and suppress weeds—though on very stony soils, this depth could be reduced.

Plastic is not used as a mulch, because adding plastics to the soil can be very harmful; they may leach toxic chemicals into the soil as they break down. They can also take more than a thousand years to degrade.

GRAVEL GARDENS

Mineral mulches can also be used to create a specific aesthetic, for example, in a gravel garden where the look of a particular natural landscape is wanted. A range of sizes of aggregate creates a more natural effect. These generally contain planted communities at less dense spacings than traditional herbaceous borders, often using species from Mediterranean or other dry regions. A deep mulch of gravel covers the soil, and the gravel can be walked on, providing access around the plants, too.

SHEET MULCHES

Some mulches come in the form of sheets of woven fabric, often laid on fresh beds and borders, with plants positioned through incisions in the fabric. They can be made more aesthetically pleasing with a layer of decorative material, such as gravel or bark. To avoid drainage issues and surface runoff and to make sure rain and irrigation water access the roots, use a permeable sheet material. Temporary sheet mulches, such as biodegradable cardboard, are also useful to control invasive weeds before a garden planted.

WHEN TO MULCH?

The best times to apply mulches are from mid- to late spring, while herbaceous plants are inactive and before annual weeds have started to sprout, and again in fall, as the plants are dying back. Fresh plantings can be mulched at any time, because discouraging weeds and retaining moisture will help the new plants become established.

> Mineral mulches can also be used to create a specific aesthetic, for example, in a Mediterranean gravel garden where the look and feel of a particular natural landscape is wanted. A range of sizes of aggregate creates a more natural effect.

ORGANIC GARDENING

Sarah's garden is a testament to organic principles:
it is beautiful, full of texture and color, and there is
not a whiff of chemical pesticide or fertilizer anywhere.

SARAH MEAD is head gardener at the Yeo Valley Organic Garden in Somerset, which is one of the few organically certified ornamental gardens in the UK. Built up by Sarah over the past 25 years, the Yeo Valley garden shows the positive impact of organic gardening and how working with nature benefits wildlife and biodiversity.

"

MANY PEOPLE THINK THAT "ORGANIC" ONLY REFERS TO GROWING FRUIT AND VEGGIES, BUT WHAT DOES IT MEAN TO BE SOIL ASSOCIATION CERTIFIED ORGANIC?

The farm in which the garden sits has been certified organic for more than 25 years, so it was important to us to gain the SA Certification for the entire 6½-acre (2.6-hectare) garden. Here at YOG, we aim to prove that organic horticulture can go hand in hand not just with fruit and veggie growing but also with a design-led garden that includes flower borders as well as meadows and areas of prairie-style planting.

WHY IS COMPOSTING SO IMPORTANT AT THE YEO VALLEY ORGANIC GARDEN?

The compost area of the garden is the "engine room" and we love to show it off. We work mostly on a closed circuit and consider the condition of the soil to be of paramount importance. If the soil is in good heart, we find that the rest of the garden follows. Soil health is the backbone of organic horticulture and agriculture.

WHAT KEY PRINCIPLES CAN GARDENERS TAKE FROM A GARDEN LIKE YOURS?

Plenty! Gardening organically is not an all or nothing club—we are super-keen that people get involved in any way they feel able to. It could be partaking in "No Mow May"; it could be actively feeding your birds over the winter; it could be allowing nature's predators to discover your blackfly. The size of your plot or the scale of your commitment doesn't matter—what matters is taking the first step.

Rain barrels can be aesthetically pleasing and don't need to be plastic! This one is made from natural weathering steel and has a planter on the top, adding more green to the garden.

RAINWATER HARVESTING

MAKING THE MOST OF RAINWATER NOT ONLY BENEFITS PLANTS BY GIVING THEM FRESH, NATURAL WATER, BUT IT EASES THE PRESSURE ON SEWAGE SYSTEMS AND HARD PERMEABLE SURFACES, REDUCING THE RISK OF FLOODING.

Swales—or rain gardens—are shallow, vegetated channels or pools that capture and store water, reducing the pressure on sanitary sewers by slowing the flow and keeping water in the landscape. (See pp.176–179 for the best plants for a swale.)

Rain barrels are a traditional way to collect and store water, but they can offer other functions; some have integrated features, such as planters.

There are many ways to harvest and store rainwater and slow the movement of water though a garden landscape. Sustainable drainage systems (SuDS) are essentially landscape features that act as above-ground catchment areas or drains, slowing water that moves into mains sewers, reducing pressure on the network. The SuDS features in the resilient garden are detailed on the following pages.

DOWNSPOUT

Place rocks or stones below the downspout to break the fall of the water and thus prevent soil erosion.

PLANTER

Planting on the top of the rain barrel makes it more visually appealing; choose plants that like poor soils. Water drains into the storage area below. This planter can be removed to access the unit beneath.

OVERFLOW PIPE

An overflow pipe regulates the water level in the storage area. When the water level reaches the top of the pipe, it flows into the pipe, and prevents the rain barrel from overflowing.

STORAGE AREA

Rainwater collects in the storage area. A tap allows the water to be siphoned off to be used for purposes such as watering the planting in your garden.

WATER DISCHARGE

The overflow pipe can direct water toward an area of planting or onto a permeable surface to be absorbed into the ground.

PASSIVE IRRIGATION

A BELOW-GROUND RAINWATER HARVESTING AND PASSIVE IRRIGATION SYSTEM CAN BE IMPLEMENTED UNDER A GRAVEL GARDEN, GREEN ROOF, OR DRIVEWAY.

A cellular crate system collects and stores rainwater and passively releases it into the soil through a wicking system. This can be connected to gutter downpipes that collect rainwater falling on roof surfaces.

PLANTING

Excess rainwater falling onto the planting will find its way to the reservoir for use at a later date.

OVERFLOW PIPE

An overflow pipe stops the system from flooding. This is generally connected to the sanitary sewers.

PAVING

Rainwater falls onto the paving, then runs off and drains through channels between slabs and adjacent permeable surfaces, down into the reservoir system below.

SOIL

The soil moisture is regulated by the wicking system. When it is dry, more moisture is wicked up into the soil.

IRRIGATION RESERVOIR

Water is stored in a reservoir to be used in dry conditions: when the soil becomes dry, the stored water is utilized.

WICKING MATERIAL

The wicking medium draws moisture up and into dry soil through capillary action—the liquid flows without the assistance of (or even in opposition to) external forces, such as gravity.

135

SUDS PLANTER

IN THE REAR GARDEN, THE WATER IS COLLECTED
FROM THE ROOF, WHERE IT RUNS INTO A PLANTER
THAT OVERFLOWS INTO A WILDLIFE POND.

DOWNSPOUT

The downspout should fall
straight onto the planted area.
Place rocks or stones below the
downspout to break the fall of
the water and thus prevent
soil erosion.

The water level in the pond will vary depending on
the rainfall each season. The pond could be topped
up with utility water in dry weather, but the most
sustainable option would be to fill it from rain
barrels, limiting utility water use. During periods
of heavy rainfall, excess water will be diverted into
the sanitary sewers, but its passage will be slowed
significantly by this water-saving system.

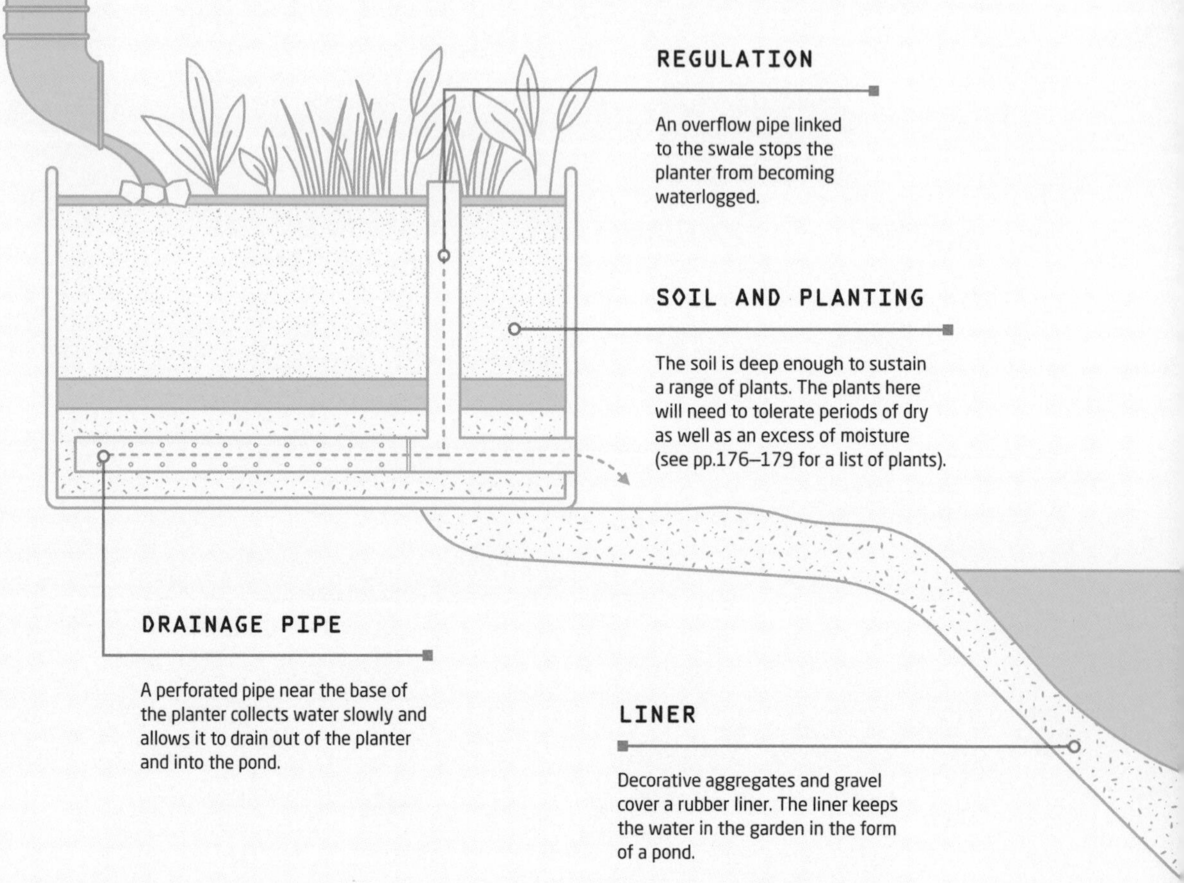

REGULATION

An overflow pipe linked
to the swale stops the
planter from becoming
waterlogged.

SOIL AND PLANTING

The soil is deep enough to sustain
a range of plants. The plants here
will need to tolerate periods of dry
as well as an excess of moisture
(see pp.176–179 for a list of plants).

DRAINAGE PIPE

A perforated pipe near the base of
the planter collects water slowly and
allows it to drain out of the planter
and into the pond.

LINER

Decorative aggregates and gravel
cover a rubber liner. The liner keeps
the water in the garden in the form
of a pond.

As well as preventing excess pressure on sanitary sewer systems, keeping water within the garden landscape brings other benefits: water adds atmosphere, sound, movement, and reflection. It bring numerous benefits for wildlife, too.

POND

The lined area creates a wildlife pond, the depth of which can be varied to suit different types of marginal and aquatic plants and the differing needs of visiting wildlife.

OVERFLOW

An overflow pipe connects to the sanitary sewers, stopping the pond from flooding during periods of excess rainfall.

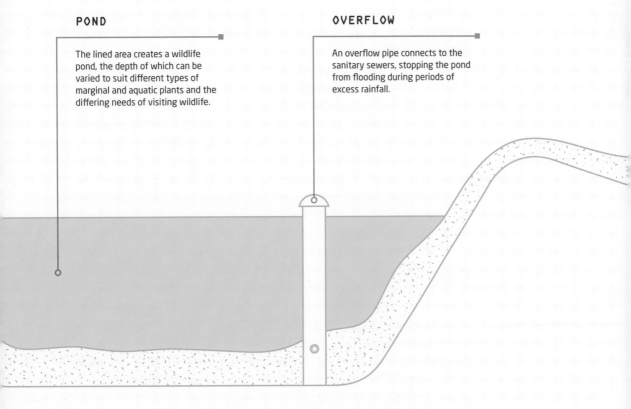

A mixed evergreen hedge windbreak makes
an attractive backdrop and a home for
wildlife as well as protecting the garden.
This dense hedge can also help reduce local
air pollution.

PROTECTIVE BOUNDARIES

IN THE RESILIENT FRONT GARDEN, A PLANTING OF MIXED EVERGREEN HEDGING SPECIES FULFILLS THE FUNCTIONS OF PROTECTING THE SPACE FROM WIND, IMPROVING AIR QUALITY BY CAPTURING POLLUTANTS FROM THE ROAD, AND PROVIDING FOOD AND SHELTER FOR WILDLIFE.

You can create a windbreak in your garden using either evergreen or deciduous plants, but make sure they are wind-resilient species for the most successful result (see pages 170–173).

WHERE TO POSITION YOUR WINDBREAK

Windbreaks should face the prevailing winds. The topography of the land will affect the wind direction; wind can gust over a hill, so a hilly site might need protection from multiple directions. Look out for wind tunnels, too. See pp.170–173 for the best species to plant for wind resistance.

PLANTING AND MAINTAINING LIVING WINDBREAKS

Deciduous shrubs and trees are best planted from fall until early spring, while evergreens should ideally be planted in spring.

- Buy small, young plants, which usually establish better in their new site than mature specimens.
- Plant shrubs and trees close together, with 1–3ft (30–90cm) between most plants within the row. If you have sufficient space, you can also plant double rows with plants staggered.
- If there are wild rabbits or deer in your area, put tree guards in place to protect the trunks from damage.
- Keep your new plantings well mulched, watered, and weed-free until they are established. Clip trees and hedges annually to keep them dense.

- While the young plants establish, a temporary screen can be installed, such as a post and porous mesh system. A more sustainable and visibly pleasing option would be a hazel hurdle or willow/bamboo screen, which will biodegrade as the hedge establishes around it.

POLLUTION CAPTURE

Plants can also assist in capturing particulate pollution. Evergreen species are best for this, as they retain their leaves year-round, providing a longer period of protection. Other qualities to look for are rough, hairy leaves and dense foliage. It should be noted that planting is only considered the third line of defense against air pollution: reducing emissions and moving farther from the source of emissions are both considered more effective. However, if you live near a busy road, these first two options may not be possible, so planting to protect against pollution is a sensible course of action (see pages 174–175 for an interview with Dr. Tijana Blanusa).

Choosing a mix of hedging species can provide other benefits, too; for example, plants that fruit and flower support different animals, insects, and invertebrates. A mixed hedge will do more to support biodiversity than a single-species one.

BIODIVERSE HABITATS

THINKING ABOUT GARDENS AS SPACES WE SHARE WITH NATURE IS IMPORTANT WHEN IT COMES TO IMPROVING BIODIVERSITY AND PROTECTING LOCAL SPECIES. SEVERAL HABITATS ARE INCLUDED IN THE RESILIENT GARDEN: NATURAL WATER, ROCKS AND BOULDERS, TREES, AND EVEN THE COMPOST HEAP.

Playing with the topography of a site can add interest to a garden, as well as new habitats. The land in the existing site was flat and dull, whereas the resilient garden design has contours and different land levels. The boggy area has been turned into a swale, or rain garden, where water collects in a depression, which adds a habitat for water-loving creatures (see pages 144–145). Hugel mounds create raised beds with rich soils, providing habitats for numerous organisms (see pages 146–147).

Hidden and protected spaces in the landscape encourage biodiversity by increasing the surface area of the garden. They also help achieve a natural effect while creating a richer and more biodiverse landscape.

Trees, especially native species, benefit wildlife, too: fruit, leaves, and flowers provide food, while the branches and canopy offer shelter for birds, animals, and insects.

Even the recycled gravel pathways can be habitat: insects and other small creatures are able to find homes in the gaps between the aggregate materials. Using a range of sizes creates habitats for a variety of species. Gaps in brick and stone walls also offer opportunities for insect life.

DEAD HEDGES

Dead hedges are stacks of brushwood and cuttings that provide a place to store woody waste as it slowly breaks down. This is also a good way of using anything that is too woody to go on the compost heap. Arranging them as deliberate structures in the garden can provide windbreaks and habitats for wildlife, as well as some fun—they can be made to look like a giant bird's nest, for example.

[Left] A habitat panel (see pp.142–143) has been installed on the side of the garden office, making use of the otherwise dead space and providing shelter for bees, beetles, spiders, and other invertebrates.

[Below] A stack of tree branch offcuts makes up a dead hedge, laid in a decorative way and notched between recycled steel beams.

HOW TO CREATE A WILDLIFE HABITAT PANEL

The resilient garden includes three habitat wildlife panels: on the side of the bin store, on the boundary fences in the rear garden, and attached to the side of the garden office. These are an effective way of inviting local species into your garden and are easy to make utilizing waste materials.

Be creative in your choices and incorporate any organic waste materials from the garden, then see which creatures come to visit. However, be careful about including kitchen or food waste, as this may attract vermin such as rats.

Here are some ideas of materials to include, depending on what you want to attract:

- Dead wood and bark for beetles, centipedes, spiders, and woodlice.
- Small holes for solitary bees, made from bamboo, reeds, and drilled logs.
- Larger holes with stones and tiles, providing cool, damp conditions for frogs and toads. Place the holes deep and low down within the structure so that they provide a frost-free home during winter.
- A variety of dry leaves, sticks, or straw for ladybugs (predator to aphids) and beetles.
- Corrugated cardboard for lacewings, whose larvae eat aphids.
- Dry leaves and leaf mulch (held in place with chicken wire) to mimic a natural forest floor.

STEP 1: CHOOSE A SUITABLE SITE

The visitors to your site will depend upon the location of your habitat panels. Solitary bees, for example, prefer a sunny location, whereas frogs and toads like cool, damp conditions that are also favored by potentially less desirable slugs and snails. However, frogs and toads eat them, so they provide an important food source.

STEP 2: CHOOSE A HARD BASE

For the basic structure, you will need a strong, stable framework. This could be made from steel, timber, or an old wooden pallet. In the resilient garden, the habitat panels on the boundary fences, the garden office, and the bin store are timber-framed, with a wire mesh cover to hold in the plant material. It's best not to use plastic for this, as it is not biodegradable.

STEP 3: ADD YOUR MATERIAL

The idea is to provide a very porous habitat with gaps, crevices, tunnels, and nooks and crannies of different sizes for wildlife to explore and make use of.

WILDLIFE PONDS

PONDS ARE ONE OF SEVERAL AREAS THAT ENCOURAGE WILDLIFE INTO THE GARDEN, INCLUDING PREDATORS THAT WILL ACT AS NATURAL CONTROL FOR LESS DESIRABLE VISITORS THAT MAY HARM OR DECIMATE PLANTS.

One of the benefits of including a natural pond in the garden is that the change in topography gives you an opportunity to plant aquatic and marginal plants, providing habitats for both aquatic and amphibious species. You can also use a pond to collect rainwater (see pp.136–137).

ENCOURAGING PREDATORS

Predators in the garden not only boost biodiversity and help plug gaps in the local ecosystem, they are also an environmentally friendly way of dealing with creatures such as slugs, snails, aphids, and caterpillars.

Adding a swale or wildlife pond will attract amphibians such as newts, frogs, and toads, which predate on slugs and snails. You can also place bird feeders in trees: birds eat slugs, snails, and caterpillars, especially during spring when they are feeding their young. Habitat panels encourage useful insects and invertebrates: ladybugs eat aphids, so they are a beneficial insect to attract.

SLUGS AND SNAILS

Slugs and snails are no longer classed as serious pests in the UK by the Royal Horticultural Society. This is part of a shift in thinking about how we perceive the wildlife in our gardens, including less popular species which still play a role in the garden ecosystem. To lessen the damage they do:
• Pick slugs and snails off your plants and move them to the compost heap, where they will help turn waste into compost.
• Place sacrificial plants near your favorite plants so they eat those instead.
• Slugs love vulnerable young seedlings, so transfer plants into the garden only once they are mature. Place cloches over vulnerable plants for protection—these can be made from recycled items such as jars or plastic bottles.

Spot the frog! Providing shelter in water through aquatic and marginal planting will encourage beneficial predators, such as toads and frogs, to inhabit your garden.

145

HUGELKULTUR MOUNDS

HUGELKULTUR IS AN ANCIENT TECHNIQUE IN WHICH DECAYING WOOD AND OTHER ORGANIC MATTER IS PILED UP AND THEN COVERED WITH SOIL AND COMPOST, CREATING A MOUND. AS THE WOOD AT THE CORE OF THE MOUND BREAKS DOWN, IT EMANATES HEAT, WARMING THE SOIL AND PROVIDING NUTRIENTS AND MOISTURE FOR THE PLANTS.

BUILDING A HUGELKULTUR MOUND

Start by clearing your selected area, removing turf or vegetation. Then follow the steps below to build your mound.

ADD SMALLER, LIGHTER WOOD MATERIALS

Smaller rotting logs, branches, twigs, and so forth help form the structure of the bed.

FILL GAPS WITH COMPOSTED BARK MULCH OR WOOD CHIPS

The chipped woody matter adds essential nutrients more quickly than the larger logs. It also absorbs moisture better.

ADD DECAYING WOOD

Wood that has fallen or been cut down at least two to three years earlier is best.

DIG UP EXISTING TURF

In the resilient garden, some of the turf of the old lawn was reused to create this hugelkultur mound. Keeping some soil on the turf adds weight to compress the timber part of the bed.

146

A hugel mound covered in vegetation; the topography of the structure also adds interest to the garden, transforming what was a flat lawn into a dynamic contoured landscape rich in biodiversity.

ADD NITROGEN-RICH MATTER

It's vital to include a layer of nitrogen-rich organic matter, so add the turf upside down to stop grass from growing up through the soil. The weight of the turf compacts the materials, aiding decay. Rotting hay, leaf mold, or grass clippings can be used as an alternative.

ADD TOPSOIL AND RICH COMPOST

The deeper the soil, the more choices you will have about what you can plant.

ADD PLANTS

See pp.180–197 for edimental and forest garden planting ideas. Note: Plants that like very dry, infertile soil conditions, such as Mediterranean herbs, will not be suitable here.

ADD MULCH

This is to protect the soil, suppress weeds, and lock in moisture. Use organic, biodegradable material (see pp.126–127).

RECLAIMED MATERIALS

THE LIGHT-TOUCH INTERVENTION ETHOS APPLIES NOT JUST TO PLANTING AND MAINTENANCE, BUT EXTENDS TO HARD LANDSCAPING IN A GARDEN, TOO. USING RECLAIMED MATERIALS CAN BRING CHARACTER AND TEXTURE TO THE AREAS OF THE GARDEN WE USE THE MOST.

HARD MATERIALS

As our gardens must cater to human use, we need to add practical hard landscaping to suit our desired function, whether that's moving easily through the space, cooking, dining, or relaxing. Applying the light-touch ethos here, materials that weather and age well avoid the need for regular maintenance. Low-impact, minimal, and permeable paving solutions allow water to pass through and be absorbed into the landscape instead of running over it and into storm drains.

Reclaimed materials should be used and championed wherever possible, and they don't need to look shabby. Reclaimed timber, for example, can be full of character and texture. It has been used for the boardwalk in the resilient garden, which floats over the space.

Other materials have also been reused in the resilient garden: the recycled aggregate gravel has been used for pathways, on the biodegradable roof of the office, and as a gravel mulch in the front garden—celebrating and enhancing material otherwise destined for landfills. The terrazzo paving was made from rubble, then polished to reveal the intricate details and textures. With creative thinking and careful processing, waste can be beautiful, too.

As our gardens must cater to human use, we need to add practical hard landscaping to suit our desired function, whether that's moving easily through the space, cooking, dining, or relaxing.

WABI-SABI

Wabi-sabi is an ideology ubiquitous across Japanese art practices and traditional aesthetics. It is centered on the practice of embracing that which is imperfect and ephemeral and can be used to describe the "imperfect, impermanent, and incomplete" beauty to be found in the natural world. Characteristics of wabi-sabi aesthetics include simplicity, asymmetry, intimacy, roughness, modesty, austerity, irregularity, coarseness, and the appreciation of both natural objects and the forces of nature.

In the resilient garden, materials such as recycled rubble terrazzo, rusty steel, and reclaimed timber contain many of the qualities admired in wabi-sabi ideology; the imperfection, weathering, and aging add beauty. The wild feeling of the planting with a lack of overly controlled form also celebrates the uncontrollable natural world. Nature does not conform to human ideals of perfection, and this is celebrated in the design.

[Top] A timber boardwalk "floats" through the garden, its raised structure allowing plants and wildlife to move beneath. [Right] Leaving channels and gaps in paved surfaces allows for better drainage and opportunities to plant the gaps. Here, creeping thyme will tolerate some foot traffic and releases scent when stepped on.

01

USING RESOURCES

In the resilient garden, the dead wood in the existing garden is seen as a resource, not as waste material to be removed. This wood is used in several ways: in the hugelkultur mound, as a bench, to grow mushrooms, and as wildlife habitats.

Dead wood is important, as it provides food and habitats for many species of woodland animals, invertebrates, plants, and fungi. Keeping dead wood within a landscape or garden instead of perceiving it to be untidy and removing it increases habitat diversity and provides niches that are warmer, damper, and more stable than many surrounding habitats.

SAPROPHYTIC FUNGI

Of the many thousands of fungi species across the world, only a small number afflict plants or animals with disease. These are called pathogenic fungi. Most species of fungi are saprophytic, meaning they gain nourishment by absorbing dead organic matter, which is an essential step in the natural process of breaking it down; they are harmless and often beneficial to their environment.

[01] The heart wood of the dead ash tree has been used as sculptural block seating. Over time, these blocks will decay and return to the landscape, but before that happens, they will provide a function. [02] Some of the timber has been sawn to create a dining table and bench set with the bark left on, creating a textural and "raw" or "live" edge. [03] Bits of brush, twigs, and waste chunks of timber are perfect for creating habitat panels. Here, they have been added to the side of the bin store, boosting its ecological function.

02

03

ASH DIEBACK

A chronic fungal disease, ash dieback has caused widespread damage to ash tree populations across Europe for 20 years. It is set to kill approximately 80 percent of the ash trees in the UK and has wiped out 90 percent of the ash trees in Denmark. This will have a devastating impact, irrevocably altering the landscape and jeopardizing the insect, animal, and bird species reliant on the ash tree, as well as having a huge economic effect, costing millions in the managing and felling of dead trees.

Quick facts
• Common disease name: Ash dieback, *Chalara*
• Scientific pathogen name: *Hymenoscyphus fraxineus*, formerly known as *Chalara fraxinea*
• Origin: East Asia, introduced to UK
• Species affected: Ash (*Fraxinus* species), especially the UK's native ash species (*F. excelsior*)
• Areas affected: Across the UK, Asia, and continental Europe

MUSHROOM LOGS

GROWING MUSHROOMS IS ONE OF THE BEST WAYS TO USE DEAD WOOD, AND IT IS EASIER THAN IT SOUNDS, ALTHOUGH IT DOES REQUIRE PATIENCE. MANY SUPPLIERS OFFER DIY KITS WITH EVERYTHING YOU NEED FOR THIS PROCESS.

HOW TO GROW A SHIITAKE MUSHROOM LOG

Shiitake (*Lentinula edodes*) is a wood-rotting fungus that grows on hardwood logs—beech, oak, and birch are particularly suitable. This mushroom is a good choice, as it is strong, quick to colonize logs and outcompete other fungi, and you can reliably induce logs to fruit as and when you want them. You can purchase wooden dowels or plugs inoculated with shiitake mushroom spawn.

STEP 1

First, select a log that has been felled from a healthy tree, approximately 3¼ft (1m) long and 4–8in (10–20cm) in diameter, and free of infection by other fungi to avoid competition.

The log should produce a minimum of one flush per year for several years, dependent on the size and density of the log and the environmental conditions. Very hard woods such as oak (*Quercus* species) can produce mushrooms for up to 10 years, while softer woods—for example, willow (*Salix* species)—may only produce for 5 years.

STEP 2

Store the log for two weeks so that the natural fungi defenses break down. Place it off the ground, sheltered from drying winds and direct sunlight to keep it from drying out too much.

STEP 3

Drill holes in the log to match the size of your mushroom plugs—usually ½in (1cm) wide and 1½in (4cm) deep. Make holes every 4–6in (10–15cm) along the length of the log. Soaking the log overnight beforehand may make drilling easier. Rotate the log and drill another series of holes in an offset diamond pattern. Aim for 50 offset holes around the log.

STEP 4

To inoculate the logs, insert the mushroom plugs into the holes with a mallet or hammer. A snug fit helps the mycelium (root system) move from the plug to the wood.

STEP 5

It is good practice to seal the holes with a layer of wax, which seals in moisture and stops competing fungi from entering the log. Daub on the wax with a brush, to the thickness of a fingernail. Soy wax is a good choice, as it has a low melting point; wax that is too hot will kill the mycelium.

STEP 6

The next step is incubation. Mushroom spawn will work its way through the log and digest the nutrients, preparing for fruiting. Incubation takes at least one spring/summer season, between 6 and 36 months. It is affected by many factors, including wood type and size and the species of mushroom.

STEP 7

If you have inoculated multiple logs that are less than 3¼ft (1m) long, you can stack them using the common method of crib stacking. Raise them off the ground on blocks or a pallet and stack them in a crisscross formation that creates an open structure for air flow, keeping the logs away from contamination by other fungi.

STEP 8

As the fungus colonizes the log, white mycelium should appear. The mycelium works its way up and down the vessels in the wood. When it turns a chocolate-brown color and the logs develop an earthy smell, they are ready to fruit.

STEP 9

The mushrooms then need to be activated, or "shocked." This mimics the log falling from a tree. The best time to shock the log is spring or fall; summer is too hot and winter is too cold, so the mycelium are dormant. Bang the log on hard ground or knock it at each end with a lump hammer.

STEP 10

Submerge the log in cold water for one to two days, ideally in a natural pond or rain barrel—avoid chemically treated water. This may not be necessary if there has been heavy rainfall.

STEP 11

After the log is removed from the water, mushroom primordia will begin to form. If conditions are reliably moist, these will quickly develop into mushroom fruiting bodies (which are very desirable to slugs and snails, so take care where you leave the logs).

STEP 12

The fruits (mushrooms) can double in size daily. In warm weather, there is a risk they will dry out, so keep them out of direct sunlight and mist the fruit with a hand mister or hose on a mist setting.

After fruiting, try shocking the log again, as this can often induce an extra flush of growth.

SOUNDSCAPE

The sound of rustling leaves, moving water, and swaying grasses can be relaxing, and dampens loud and stress-inducing city noises such as traffic, sirens, trains, and airplanes.

WILDLIFE

Wildlife is being encouraged into the garden; seeing wildlife lifts the spirits and reminds us that we share the planet with other forms of life.

CONNECTING WITH NATURE

THE RESILIENT GARDEN HAS BEEN DESIGNED SO THAT ITS INHABITANTS WILL DEEPEN THEIR CONNECTION WITH NATURE, WHICH IS VITAL TO HUMAN WELL-BEING. IN AN INCREASINGLY HECTIC WORLD, PARKS, GARDENS, AND NATURAL LANDSCAPES ARE USED AS PLACES OF RESPITE—AN ESCAPE FROM THE STRESSES AND PRESSURES OF DAILY EXISTENCE.

TREES

Trees cool and protect the space from the hot sun by casting dappled shade.

FOOD FOREST

Immersive, interactive, and sensory, it is planted with forageable species.

SOFT LANDSCAPING

Plants cover the soil and vertical surfaces, such as fences, outbuildings, and walls, softening the landscape.

THE VIEW

The plants are close to both the house and the outbuilding, meaning they are visible from indoors, enhancing the connection between the inside and outside spaces.

The BBC podcast Forest 404, which explores what it would mean to have a world without nature, discovered in a collaborative study that sounds in nature may have a positive impact on our mental health. Some 7,500 participants were played sounds from different landscapes, from English coastlines and woodlands to Papua New Guinea's tropical rainforests. The study found that stress and mental fatigue were alleviated by the sounds of birdsong. Participants described therapeutic benefits after listening to sounds such as rainfall or breaking waves. When these natural sounds were omitted, participants reported a decrease in the beneficial psychological effects, and their desire to preserve the planet's ecosystems decreased.

Alex Smalley, the principal researcher from the University of Exeter, said, "If we hope to harness nature's health benefits in the future, we need to ensure everyone has opportunities to foster positive experiences with the natural world today."

CHAPTER FIVE

RESILIENT PLANT GUIDE

Gravel garden: plants
that are resistant
to drought and wind.
Planted pathways:
permeable channels
for water to drain.
Hedges and trees:
a means of trapping
pollution particulates
and cooling the space.

GUIDE TO
RESILIENT PLANTS

THE DESIGN OF THE RESILIENT GARDEN ENCOMPASSES SEVERAL AREAS,
EACH WITH DIFFERENT CHARACTERISTICS THAT DEMONSTRATE HOW
PLANTS CAN IMPROVE THE HUMAN EXPERIENCE OF A SPACE BY ADDING
ATMOSPHERE AND CHARACTER, AS WELL AS PRACTICAL BENEFITS.

Apart from their aesthetic appeal, planting schemes
can benefit the environment by functioning as
ecological, self-sustaining communities that provide
food and shelter for wildlife, increase biodiversity,
clean the air, and lock carbon into the soil. This
chapter lists plants that are likely to survive and
thrive in challenging conditions. The plants included
in the resilient garden design in Chapter 4 are
listed here, along with other similar plants that
have characteristics that make them resilient
performers in a garden setting. For an explanation
of the hardiness ratings, see page 247.

REAR GARDEN

Swale planting: species that can tolerate fluctuating wet and dry conditions. Forest garden: ornamental and edible plants that coexist ecologically in a layered scheme, including ground-cover, climbers, shrubs, and trees. Plants for a green roof: species that require little or no active watering for living roof systems.

PLANTING ICONS

 Drought-resilient
Plants may have deep root systems, and fleshy/waxy, narrow, or grey, hairy leaves.

 Wind-resilient
Plants have fine or waxy leaves, flexible stems, or branches that wont break easily in high winds.

 Plants for pollinators
May have open flowers that offer easy access, or provide a high quantity of nectar or pollen.

 Edimental
Plants with ornamental qualities and edible parts—for example, flowers or fruit.

 Pollution-reducing
Plants may be dense and evergreen or have hairy, or rough leaves good at trapping particulates.

 Resilience to waterlogging
Species that will tolerate periods of waterlogged soil.

GRAVEL GARDEN

THE GRAVELED AREA IN THE FRONT GARDEN INCLUDES DROUGHT- AND WIND-RESISTANT PLANTING WITH LOW, CREEPING PLANTS EXTENDING INTO THE DRIVEWAY. THE MIX ALSO HAS HIGH VISUAL AND SENSORY APPEAL, WITH PLENTY OF COLOR, SCENT, AND TEXTURE.

01 *Hesperaloe parviflora*

A yuccalike perennial, forming clumps of arching, linear, leathery leaves. In summer, flower spikes up to 5ft (1.5m) long bear tubular to bell-shaped pink flowers. It can take extreme cold and tolerates drought.

Common name Small-flowered hesperaloe **Foliage** Evergreen **Height** 3¼–5ft (1–1.5m) **Spread** 2–4in (5–10cm) **Exposure** Full sun, sheltered **Soil** Well-drained loam, sand (acid/neutral) **Hardiness** Zones 8–9

02 *Euphorbia rigida*

An erect, then spreading, evergreen perennial. The blue-green leaves are fleshy and arranged spirally. Bright yellow flowers appear in small clusters at the tips of the shoots in late spring and early summer.

Common name Spurge **Foliage** Evergreen **Height** 4–20in (10–50cm) **Spread** 4–20in (10–50cm) **Exposure** Full sun or partial shade, exposed or sheltered **Soil** Well-drained/moist but well-drained chalk, clay, loam, sand (acid/alkaline/neutral) **Hardiness** Zones 6–7

03 *Salvia greggii*

A bushy dwarf shrub, branching from the base and evergreen if not cut back by frosts, with small, aromatic, mid- to deep green leaves. Red, purple, pink, yellow, or violet flowers appear from late summer to fall. A highly fragrant border for pathways.

Common name Autumn sage **Foliage** Evergreen **Height** 20–39in (50–100cm) **Spread** 20–39in (50–100cm) **Exposure** Full sun, sheltered **Soil** Well-drained/moist but well-drained chalk, loam, sand (acid/alkaline/neutral) **Hardiness** Zones 8–9

04 *Thymus serpyllum 'Elfin'*

An evergreen subshrub, 'Elfin' forms a dense mound of trailing stems with small, aromatic, gray-green leaves and small, lilac-pink flowers in summer. It releases scent when brushed against or stepped on, so it is great between gaps in paving. The aromatic leaves are used in cooking.

Common name Thyme 'Elfin' **Foliage** Evergreen **Height** 4in (10cm) **Spread** 4–20in (10–50cm) **Exposure** Full sun, exposed or sheltered **Soil** Well-drained chalk, loam, sand (alkaline/neutral) **Hardiness** Zones 7–8

05 *Stachys byzantina*

A carpeting, evergreen perennial, with thick, soft, oblong-elliptic leaves that are densely white-woolly. The flowers are purplish or pink, sometimes striped, borne in whorls in an interrupted spike in summer. The leaves can be deep-fried, known colloquially as "poor man's fish."

Common name Lamb's ear **Foliage** Evergreen
Height 4–20in (10–50cm) **Spread** 20–39in (50–100cm) **Exposure** Full sun, exposed
Soil Well-drained chalk, loam, sand (acid/alkaline/neutral) **Hardiness** Zone 6

06 *Stipa tenuissima*

A deciduous grass, forming a compact upright tuft of threadlike leaves, with narrow, arching, feathery flowering panicles in summer.

Common name Mexican feather grass
Foliage Deciduous **Height** 20–39in (50–100cm)
Spread 4–20in (10–50cm) **Exposure** Full sun, exposed or sheltered **Soil** Well-drained/moist but well-drained chalk, clay, loam, sand
Hardiness Zones 8–9

07 *Pinus mugo* 'Mops'

'Mops' is a slow-growing evergreen conifer that makes a medium-sized shrub of bushy, rounded habit, with slender, paired, dark green needles. Its dense evergreen foliage is good at capturing particulate pollution.

Common name Dwarf mountain pine 'Mops'
Foliage Evergreen **Height** 20–39in (50–100cm)
Spread 20–39in (50–100cm) **Exposure** Full sun, exposed or sheltered **Soil** Well-drained chalk, clay, loam, sand (acid/alkaline/neutral)
Hardiness Zone 6

08 *Salvia rosmarinus*

This bushy shrub has linear, dark green leaves that are used to flavor food. Its pale violet and white flowers bloom mainly in spring and summer.

Common name Rosemary **Foliage** Evergreen **Height** 5–8ft (1.5–2.5m) **Spread** 5–8ft (1.5–2.5m) **Exposure** Full sun, exposed or sheltered **Soil** Well-drained/moist but well-drained chalk, clay, loam, sand (acid/alkaline/neutral) **Hardiness** Zones 8–9

09 *Lavandula stoechas*

An aromatic dwarf shrub, with narrow, gray-green leaves and short-stalked, dense heads of tiny, deep purple flowers topped by a tuft of purple bracts.

Common name French lavender **Foliage** Evergreen **Height** 20–39in (50–100cm) **Spread** 20–39in (50–100cm) **Exposure** Full sun, sheltered **Soil** Well-drained chalk, loam, sand (acid/alkaline/neutral) **Hardiness** Zones 8–9

10 *Helichrysum italicum*

A small bushy evergreen subshrub with linear, silvery-gray, curry-scented leaves and small yellow flowerheads in domed clusters. The potently scented leaves can be used to add a "curry" flavor to food.

Common name Curry plant **Foliage** Evergreen **Height** 4–20in (10–50cm) **Spread** 20–39in (50–100cm) **Exposure** Full sun, sheltered **Soil** Well-drained chalk, loam (alkaline/neutral) **Hardiness** Zones 8–9

Nepeta racemosa 'Little Titch'

A compact herbaceous perennial that forms a low carpet of aromatic foliage topped with short spikes of lavender-blue flowers in spring and summer. It is perfect as an edging plant to pathways where its scent can be enjoyed.

Common name Catmint
Foliage Deciduous
Height 4–20in (10–50cm)
Spread 4–20in (10–50cm)
Exposure Full sun, exposed or sheltered **Soil** Well-drained chalk, loam, sand (acid/alkaline/neutral)
Hardiness Zone 6

Geranium renardii

This herbaceous perennial forms clumps of lobed, wrinkled leaves. Its white or mauve flowers with violet veins bloom in summer.

Common name Renard geranium
Foliage Deciduous
Height 4–20in (10–50cm)
Spread 4–20in (10–50cm)
Exposure Full sun, partial shade, exposed or sheltered
Soil Well-drained/moist but well-drained chalk, clay, loam, sand (acid/alkaline/neutral)
Hardiness Zones 6–7

Papaver dubium subsp. *lecoqii albiflorum*

This small pink annual poppy is called "Beth's poppy" after the renowned plantswoman Beth Chatto. It can be allowed to self-sow in a sunny, well-drained site.

Common name Beth's poppy
Foliage Deciduous **Height** 16in (40cm) **Spread** 6in (15cm)
Exposure Full sun, exposed or sheltered **Soil** Well-drained light loam or sand (acid/alkaline/neutral) **Hardiness** Zone 6

Lavandula angustifolia 'Hidcote Blue'

This bushy dwarf shrub has narrow, silvery-gray leaves and dense spikes of deep violet aromatic flowers that bloom in summer.

Common name English lavender 'Hidcote'
Foliage Evergreen **Height** 4–20in (10–50cm)
Spread 20–39in (50–100cm) **Exposure** Full sun, sheltered **Soil type** Well-drained chalk, clay, loam, sand (acid/alkaline/neutral)
Hardiness Zones 7–8

Festuca glauca

An evergreen blue grass that forms in clumps and becomes greener in winter. In late spring and summer, it bears bristly blue-green flower plumes that turn golden-brown in fall.

Common name Blue fescue
Foliage Evergreen
Height 4–20in (10–50cm)
Spread 4–20in (10–50cm)
Exposure Full sun, exposed or sheltered **Soil** Well-drained/moist but well-drained chalk, loam, sand (acid/alkaline/neutral)
Hardiness Zones 7–8

Orlaya grandiflora

This branching annual has jagged leaves. In summer and fall, it has white flowers comprising a small inner flower and a ring of larger outer petals.

Common name White laceflower
Foliage Deciduous
Height 20–39in (50–100cm)
Spread 4–20in (10–50cm)
Exposure Full sun, exposed or sheltered **Soil** Well-drained chalk, loam, sand (acid/alkaline/neutral)
Hardiness Zone 6

Salvia fruticosa

This sage has paired aromatic leaves and pink flowers. It can be grown as an annual or evergreen perennial herb or herbaceous shrub and is very drought tolerant once established.

Common name Greek sage
Foliage Evergreen
Height 2–3ft (60–90cm)
Spread 26ft (8m) or more
Exposure Full sun or partial shade, exposed or sheltered
Soil Well-drained chalk, clay, loam, sand (acid/alkaline/neutral)
Hardiness Zones 8–9

Salvia nemorosa 'Ostfriesland'

This variety of Balkan sage is a compact, bushy perennial with narrow oval leaves and erect stems that bear deep violet flowers and pink bracts in summer and fall. It is popular with pollinators.

Common name Balkan clary **Foliage** Deciduous
Height 4–20in (10–50cm) **Spread** 4–20in (10–50cm) **Exposure** Full sun, exposed or sheltered **Soil type** Well-drained chalk, loam, sand (acid/alkaline/neutral)
Hardiness Zone 6

Eschscholzia californica

A bushy annual or biennial plant, California poppy has blue-green leaves and yellow, orange, or red flowers that bloom in summer. It will seed into hostile environments such as gaps in paving or walls.

Common name California poppy
Foliage Deciduous
Height 4–20in (10–50cm)
Spread 4–20in (10–50cm)
Exposure Full sun, exposed or sheltered **Soil** Well-drained chalk, loam, sand (acid/alkaline/neutral)
Hardiness Zones 9–10

Salvia officinalis

This dwarf bushy shrub has aromatic, gray-green leaves that are used for culinary purposes and short spikes of pale blue flowers in early summer.

Common name Common sage **Foliage** Evergreen
Height 20–39in (50–100cm)
Spread 20–39in (50–100cm)
Exposure Full sun or partial shade, sheltered **Soil** Well-drained clay, loam (acid/alkaline/neutral)
Hardiness Zones 7–8

Eryngium ebracteatum

An erect herbaceous perennial with spiny gray-green leaves and wiry stems, this eryngium has red-brown flowerheads that bloom in summer and fall.

Common name Burnet-flowered sea holly, thrift
Foliage Evergreen **Height** 3¼–5ft (1–1.5m) **Spread** 1½–3¼ft (0.5–1m) **Exposure** Full sun, exposed or sheltered
Soil Well-drained chalk, loam, sand (acid/alkaline/neutral)
Hardiness Zones 8–9

Centranthus ruber

This woody herbaceous perennial or biennial bears dense clusters of fragrant pink or white flowers from late spring to fall. It is often seen growing on drystone walls.

Common name Red valerian
Foliage Semievergreen **Height** 20–39in (50–100cm) **Spread** 4–20in (10–50cm)
Exposure Full sun, exposed **Soil** Well-drained chalk, loam, sand (alkaline/neutral)
Hardiness Zones 6–7

Asphodeline lutea

A herbaceous perennial, asphodel has narrow leaves and fragrant, cheerful yellow flowers that bloom in late spring.

Common name Asphodel **Foliage** Evergreen **Height** 3¼–6ft (1–1.5m) **Spread** 4–20in (10–50cm) **Exposure** Full sun, exposed or sheltered **Soil** Well-drained chalk, loam, sand (acid/alkaline/neutral) **Hardiness** Zones 8–9

Calamintha nepeta

A compact, bushy perennial, this plant has aromatic leaves and loose clusters of tiny, tubular white or lilac flowers from summer to early fall.

Common name Lesser calamint
Foliage Semievergreen **Height** 20–39in (50–100cm) **Spread** 20–39in (50–100cm)
Exposure Full sun, exposed or sheltered
Soil Well-drained chalk, loam, sand (alkaline/ neutral) **Hardiness** Zones 7–8

Thymus vulgaris

A popular culinary herb, common thyme forms a bushy dwarf shrub with aromatic leaves. Spikes of small, whorled, white or pink flowers appear in early summer.

Common name Common thyme **Foliage** Evergreen **Height** 4–20in (10–50cm) **Spread** 4–20in (10–50cm) **Exposure** Full sun, exposed or sheltered **Soil** Well-drained chalk, loam, sand (alkaline/neutral) **Hardiness** Zones 7–8

Echium vulgare

An erect, bristly biennial with long, hairy leaves and cylindrical spikes of bell-shaped electric-blue flowers that appear in early summer—a magnet for pollinators.

Common name Viper's bugloss
Foliage Deciduous
Height 20–39in (50–100cm)
Spread 4–20in (10–50cm)
Exposure Full sun, exposed or sheltered **Soil** Well-drained chalk, loam, sand (acid/alkaline/neutral)
Hardiness Zone 6

Erigeron karvinskianus

This herbaceous perennial forms mats with delicate leaves and white daisy flowers in summer that turn pink. It self-seeds profusely.

Common name Mexican fleabane
Foliage Semievergreen
Height 4–20in (10–50cm)
Spread 20–39in (50–100cm)
Exposure Full sun, exposed
Soil Well-drained chalk, clay, loam, sand (acid/alkaline/neutral)
Hardiness Zones 7–8

Thymus pseudolanuginosus

This edible herb is a fragrant, creeping subshrub that forms mats of small leaves fringed with minute hairs and produces purple flowers in summer.

Common name Wild thyme
Foliage Evergreen **Height** 4in (10cm) **Spread** 4–20in (10–50cm)
Exposure Full sun, exposed or sheltered **Soil** Well-drained chalk, loam, sand (alkaline/neutral)
Hardiness Zones 7–8

Hordeum jubatum

A tufted annual or perennial grass producing long, silky bristles with tips that turn red in summer. It is very tactile and textural.

Common name Foxtail barley
Foliage Deciduous **Height** 20–39in (50–100cm) **Spread** 4–20in (10–50cm) **Exposure** Full sun, exposed or sheltered **Soil** Well-drained chalk, clay, loam, sand (acid/alkaline/neutral)
Hardiness Zones 6–7

HEDGES AND TREES

THESE PLANTS HAVE BEEN CHOSEN MAINLY TO REDUCE POLLUTION AND TRAFFIC NOISE, BUT ALSO TO PROVIDE A VISUAL SCREEN, SHELTER AND FOOD FOR WILDLIFE, AND AREAS OF SHADE IN A GARDEN.

01 *Pinus sylvestris*

A very wind-resistant evergreen tree, with orange-brown branches and upper trunk and a picturesque outline with age. The twisted gray-green needles are borne in pairs.

Common name Scots pine **Foliage** Evergreen **Height** 59ft (12m) or more **Spread** 26ft (8m) or more **Exposure** Full sun, exposed or sheltered **Soil** Well-drained chalk, clay, loam, sand (acid/alkaline/neutral) **Hardiness** Zone 6

02 *Pinus sylvestris* 'Watereri'

A small, slow-growing form of Scots pine, often multistemmed, with flaky brown bark and pairs of blue-green needles, 'Watereri' bears cones throughout the year.

Common name Scots pine 'Watereri' **Foliage** Evergreen **Height** 8–13ft (2.5–4m) **Spread** 13–26ft (4–8m) **Exposure** Full sun, exposed or sheltered **Soil** Well-drained chalk, clay, loam, sand (acid/alkaline/neutral) **Hardiness** Zone 6

03 *Callistemon viminalis* 'Captain Cook'

This dense, round shrub has narrow leaves and bright red, bottle brush-shaped flowers that bloom from early summer to fall. The dense evergreen foliage is good for screening and providing some protection against air pollutants.

Common name Bottlebrush 'Captain Cook' **Foliage** Evergreen
Height 5–8ft (1.5–2.5m)
Spread 5–8ft (1.5–2.5m)
Exposure Full sun, sheltered
Soil Moist but well-drained clay, loam, sand (acid/neutral)
Hardiness Zones 9–10

04 *Cotoneaster franchetii*

A tall shrub with arching branches and glossy leaves that trap particulates, this cotoneaster bears clusters of white flowers tinged with pink in early summer, followed by orange fruits in fall and winter.

Common name Franchet's cotoneaster **Foliage** Evergreen
Height 8–13ft (2.5–4m)
Spread 8–13ft (2.5–4m)
Exposure Full sun or partial shade, exposed or sheltered
Soil Well-drained/moist but well-drained chalk, clay, loam, sand (acid/alkaline/neutral)
Hardiness Zones 6–7

Sorbus aria

This medium-sized, upright tree has oval, dark green leaves and clusters of white flowers in spring that are followed by red berries in early fall.

Common name Common whitebeam
Foliage Deciduous **Height** 26–39ft (8–12m)
Spread 13–26ft (4–8m) **Exposure** Full sun or partial shade, exposed or sheltered
Soil Well-drained/moist but well-drained chalk, clay, loam, sand (acid/alkaline/neutral) **Hardiness** Zones 6–7

Taxus baccata

Yew forms a medium-sized bushy tree with narrow, dark green leaves but can be pruned to form a very dense hedge. The spring flowers are followed by fleshy red fruits in fall on female plants.

Common name Common yew
Foliage Evergreen
Height 39ft (12m) or more
Spread 26ft (8m) or more
Exposure Full shade to full sun, exposed or sheltered
Soil Well-drained chalk, clay, loam, sand (acid/alkaline/neutral)
Hardiness Zone 6

Phillyrea angustifolia

A compact shrub with narrow, dark green leaves, mock privet has small clusters of fragrant white flowers in late spring and early summer, followed by blue fruits in fall.

Common name Narrow-leaved mock privet
Foliage Evergreen **Height** 8–13ft (2.5–4m) **Spread** 5–8ft (1.5–2.5m)
Exposure Full sun, partial shade, exposed or sheltered
Soil Well-drained sand, loam (acid/alkaline/neutral)
Hardiness Zones 7–8

Elaeagnus angustifolia

This spreading shrub has spiky, red shoots and dark-green oval leaves. The fragrant yellow summer flowers are followed by yellow fruits in fall.

Common name Bohemian oleaster
Foliage Deciduous **Height** 13–26ft (4–8m)
Spread 13–26ft (4–8m) **Exposure** Full sun, exposed or sheltered **Soil type** Well-drained/moist but well-drained chalk, clay, loam, sand (acid/alkaline/neutral) **Hardiness** Zones 7–8

Quercus ilex

A large tree that develops a rounded crown, the holm oak has black bark; glossy, dark, oval-shaped leaves; and yellow catkins in spring, followed by fall acorns. It can be pruned and trained into formal shapes.

Common name Holm oak
Foliage Evergreen **Height** 39ft (12m) or more **Spread** 26ft (8m) or more **Exposure** Full sun or partial shade, exposed or sheltered **Soil** Well-drained/moist but well-drained chalk, clay, loam, sand (acid/alkaline/neutral)
Hardiness Zones 8–9

Genista aetnensis

A large shrub or small tree with arching green shoots and small, sparse leaves, Mount Etna broom bears bright yellow, fragrant, pea-shaped flowers in summer, followed by fruits in fall.

Common name Mount Etna broom
Foliage Deciduous **Height** 13–26ft (4–8m)
Spread 13–26ft (4–8m) **Exposure** Full sun, exposed or sheltered **Soil** Well-drained chalk, clay, loam, sand (acid/alkaline/neutral)
Hardiness Zones 7–8

Quercus suber

Known for its characterful cork bark, used to produce cork-based products, this slow-growing tree has dark, glossy leaves and long, slender acorns in fall.

Common name Cork oak **Foliage** Evergreen **Height** 39ft (12m) or more **Spread** 26ft (8m) or more **Exposure** Full sun, sheltered **Soil** Well-drained loam, sand (acid/alkaline/neutral) **Hardiness** Zones 7–8

ANTI-POLLUTION PLANTS

DR. TIJANA BLANUSA is a principal scientist at the RHS and leads the Ecosystem Services Research Programme, identifying plant characteristics that might be used to benefit wider habitats and looking at the environmental value of gardens and urban green infrastructure.

In Parc Central de Poblenou in Barcelona, layers of dense vegetation are used to provide screening and protection from the adjacent city road.

"

CAN PLANTS REALLY HELP IN TRAPPING POLLUTION AND FILTERING THE AIR?

Plants can take up gaseous pollutants such as excess carbon dioxide and break them up, store them, or use them for their own metabolism. Leaves and stems can also act as surfaces onto which particulate pollution is deposited and thus removed from the air. The current scientific thinking is that plant barriers are only the third line of defense against pollution, after the reduction of pollution emissions and a greater distance to pollution sources—but the taller and deeper the barrier, the better.

ARE THERE PARTICULAR QUALITIES IN PLANTS TO LOOK OUT FOR?

Plants that have large, dense canopies are the most effective. Fast-growing, thirsty species tend to have a high level of gas exchange, indicating that they could be effective at the uptake of gaseous pollutants. Other qualities that increase particle capture are rough and hairy leaf surfaces.

HOW ELSE CAN PLANTS IMPROVE WELL-BEING IN URBAN ENVIRONMENTS?

Plants cool the air via shade and evapo-transpiration and can also insulate buildings and reduce noise levels—all of those directly affect human well-being, not to mention the psychological benefits that come from being surrounded by greenery.

SOME SPECIES ARE REFERRED TO AS "SUPER PLANTS"— SHOULD WE BE LOOKING AT THEM IN A MORE BALANCED WAY?

Yes, we should. A plant may not excel at any singular service but may offer multiple benefits by way of supporting biodiversity, reducing flooding risks, regulating a microclimate, and making urban spaces more pleasant to live in.

WHAT SHOULD THE FUTURE OF PLANTING DESIGN IN URBAN ENVIRONMENTS LOOK LIKE?

What we know currently suggests that diverse perennial planting combinations and the use of woody plants can deliver many environmental benefits. Evergreen vegetation (mixed in with deciduous) also seems [like] a way to maximize year-round environmental benefits.

SWALE PLANTING

THE PLANTS IN THE SWALE AREA AND WILDLIFE POND CAN TOLERATE SEASONAL WET AND DRY CONDITIONS. THIS AREA HAS BEEN DESIGNED TO BE FLOODED IN PERIODS OF HEAVIER RAINFALL AND TO DRY OUT WHEN RAINFALL IS SCARCE.

01 *Acorus calamus*

A spreading, tufted herbaceous perennial with aromatic, sword-shaped leaves. The raw, partially grown flower stems and the young stalks in spring are sweet and tasty eaten in a salad, while the roots have a gingery taste. It is also known as sweet rush and sweet cinnamon.

Common name Silver-striped sweet flag **Foliage** Deciduous **Height** 20–39in (50–100m) **Spread** 4–20in (10–50cm) **Exposure** Full sun, exposed or sheltered **Soil** Poorly drained clay, loam, sand (acid/alkaline/ neutral) **Hardiness** Zone 6

176

02 *Iris pseudacorus*

A vigorous herbaceous perennial, the yellow iris forms colonies of bright yellow flowers with brown veining in the center during early and midsummer. It spreads rapidly, so it can need management in a small pond.

Common name Yellow iris
Foliage Deciduous
Height 3¼–5ft (1–1.5m)
Spread 1½–3¼ft (0.5–1m)
Exposure Full sun or partial shade, exposed or sheltered
Soil Poorly drained clay, loam (acid) **Hardiness** Zone 6

03 *Lythrum salicaria*

This herbaceous perennial has upright stems; narrow, willowy leaves; and small vivid purplish-pink flowers borne in dense spikes over a long period in summer.

Common name Purple loosestrife
Foliage Deciduous
Height 3¼–5ft (1–1.5m)
Spread 4–20in (10–50cm)
Exposure Full sun, exposed or sheltered **Soil** Moist but well-drained or poorly drained clay, loam (acid/alkaline/neutral)
Hardiness Zone 6

04 *Valeriana officinalis*

Valerian is an upright herbaceous perennial, with scented pinnate leaves and rounded clusters of small pink or white flowers in summer. It is an edible plant and the ground root is used medicinally.

Common name Common valerian
Foliage Deciduous
Height 3¼–5ft (1–1.5m)
Spread 1½–3¼ft (0.5–1m)
Exposure Full sun or partial shade, exposed or sheltered
Soil type Chalk, clay, loam, sand (acid/alkaline/neutral)
Hardiness Zones 8–9

Juncus effusus

A clump-forming grasslike perennial with green to yellowish rounded stems held in arching fans, the common rush produces rounded heads of small green to brown flowers that bloom in spring and summer.

Common name Common rush **Foliage** Evergreen **Height** 3¼–5ft (1–1.5m) **Spread** 1½–3¼ft (0.5–1m) **Exposure** Full sun to full shade, exposed or sheltered **Soil type** Poorly drained clay, loam (acid) **Hardiness** Zones 6–7

Osmunda regalis

This robust fern forms a large clump of bipinnate fronds with rusty-brown spore-bearing leaflets at the tips. During fall, the foliage turns an attractive red-brown.

Common name Royal fern
Foliage Deciduous
Height 5–8ft (1.5–2.5m)
Spread 1½–3¼ft (0.5–1m)
Exposure Full sun to full shade, exposed or sheltered
Soil type Moist but well-drained/poorly drained chalk, clay, loam (acid/alkaline/neutral)
Hardiness Zones 6–7

Butomus umbellatus

A herbaceous perennial, this plant has upright, twisted grassy leaves. In late summer, it produces rosy-pink flowers on stiff stems.

Common name Flowering rush
Foliage Deciduous **Height** 3¼–5ft (1–1.5m)
Spread 4–20in (10–50cm) **Exposure** Full sun, exposed or sheltered **Soil type** Poorly drained clay, loam, sand (acid/alkaline/neutral)
Hardiness Zones 7–8

Carex divulsa

This densely tufted sedge has arching, dark green or grayish-green leaves and short spikes of greenish-brown flowers that bloom in summer. It is resilient in a range of conditions, from shade to full sun.

Common name Gray sedge
Foliage Evergreen
Height 20–39in (50–100cm)
Spread 20–39in (50–100cm)
Exposure Full sun to full shade, exposed or sheltered **Soil** Poorly drained/moist but well-drained/well-drained chalk, clay, loam, sand (acid/alkaline/neutral)
Hardiness Zones 7–8

Angelica archangelica

A robust, upright perennial, angelica has two- to three-pinnate leaves and rounded umbels of light yellow flowers in early summer. Fresh stalks and leaves can be eaten raw in fruit salads or used as a garnish. The stalks can also be stewed or candied.

Common name Angelica
Foliage Deciduous
Height 5–8ft (1.5–2.5m)
Spread 3¹/₄–5ft (1–1.5m)
Exposure Full sun or partial shade, exposed or sheltered
Soil Moist but well-drained/poorly drained chalk, clay, loam (acid/alkaline/neutral)
Hardiness Zones 6–7

Symphytum officinale

A perennial that forms a clump of erect stems bearing elliptic leaves, comfrey produces clusters of tubular bell-shaped, purple, pink, or cream flowers in late spring and summer. It can be used to make "comfrey tea," which is an organic fertilizer.

Common name Common comfrey
Foliage Deciduous
Height 3¹/₄–5ft (1–1.5m)
Spread 3¹/₄–5ft (1–1.5m)
Exposure Full sun or partial shade, exposed or sheltered
Soil type Moist but well-drained or poorly drained chalk, clay, loam, sand (acid/alkaline/neutral)
Hardiness Zone 6

FOOD FOREST

WITH PLANT TYPES OF VARYING HEIGHTS, AND EDIBLE SPECIES PROVIDING FOOD YEAR-ROUND, FOREST GARDENS OFFER GREAT USE OF SPACE FOR PLOTS THAT MAY BE TOO SMALL FOR A TRADITIONAL PRODUCTIVE AREA. THEY ALSO SUPPORT A HUGE AMOUNT OF WILDLIFE, AS MANY PLANTS WILL FLOWER, FRUIT, AND PROVIDE SHELTER.

01 *Ficus carica*

A large shrub or small, spreading tree with rounded, lobed leaves, this plant bears insignificant flowers that are followed by edible fruit that ripens to shades of green and purple in fall. The scented leaves can also be used to perfume and flavor food.

Common name Fig
Foliage Deciduous **Height** 8–13ft (2.5m–4m) **Spread** 8–13ft (2.5m–4m) **Exposure** Full sun, sheltered **Soil** Well-drained/moist but well-drained chalk, loam, sand (alkaline/neutral)
Hardiness Zones 8–9

02 *Malus sylvestris*

This small, rounded tree has ovate leaves and, in late spring, pink-flushed white blossom. This is followed by yellowish-green, sometimes red-flushed apples that can be used to make crab-apple jelly.

Common name Crab apple
Foliage Deciduous
Height 26–39ft (8–12m)
Spread 13–26ft (4–8m)
Exposure Full sun or partial shade, exposed or sheltered **Soil** Moist but well-drained chalk, clay, loam, sand (acid/alkaline/neutral)
Hardiness Zones 6–7

03 *Prunus avium*

This medium-sized deciduous tree bears clusters of pure white flowers 1in (2.5cm) wide in late spring. They are followed by small, shiny red-purple cherries that are popular with birds. For larger, sweeter fruits, opt for a cultivar such as 'Stella'.

Common name Wild cherry
Foliage Deciduous **Height** 39ft (12m) or more **Spread** 26ft (8m) or more **Exposure** Full sun, exposed or sheltered **Soil** Well-drained/ moist but well-drained chalk, clay, loam, sand (acid/alkaline/neutral)
Hardiness Zones 6–7

04 *Sorbus aucuparia*

An upright deciduous tree, the rowan has pinnate leaves that turn yellow in fall, and clusters of white flowers in late spring, followed by orange-red berries in early fall. They are acidic and best used to make jams and preserves.

Common name Rowan
Foliage Deciduous **Height** 39ft (12m) or more **Spread** 13–26ft (4–8m) **Exposure** Full sun or partial shade, exposed or sheltered **Soil** Well-drained loam, sand (acid/neutral)
Hardiness Zones 6–7

05 *Cornus kousa*

This is a small, bushy tree with oval leaves that turn reddish-purple in fall. The small white flowers appear in summer. They are followed by deep pink, edible fruits that resemble strawberries.

Common name Kousa
Foliage Deciduous **Height** 13–26ft (4–8m) **Spread** 13–26ft (4–8m)
Exposure Full sun or partial shade, exposed or sheltered **Soil** Well-drained/moist but well-drained chalk, loam, sand (acid/alkaline/neutral)
Hardiness Zones 6–7

06 *Monarda* 'Cambridge Scarlet'

This herbaceous perennial grows in a clump to 36in (90cm) in height, with aromatic, edible leaves and whorls of deep scarlet, two-lipped flowers that make an edible garnish for salads.

Common name Bergamot 'Cambridge Scarlet'
Foliage Deciduous
Height 20–39in (50–100cm)
Spread 4–20in (10–50cm)
Exposure Full sun or partial shade, exposed or sheltered **Soil** Moist but well-drained chalk, clay, loam, sand (acid/alkaline/neutral)
Hardiness Zones 8–9

07 *Hemerocallis* 'Stafford'

A deciduous perennial that bears narrow-petaled deep red, fleshy flowers with yellow midribs and a yellow throat, appearing daily in midsummer. They are edible and delicious in salads.

Common name Daylily 'Stafford'
Foliage Deciduous
Height 20–39in (50–100cm)
Spread 4–20in (10–50cm)
Exposure Full sun, exposed or sheltered **Soil** Moist but well-drained chalk, clay, loam (acid/alkaline/neutral)
Hardiness Zones 6–7

08 *Hippophae rhamnoides*

A large, deciduous shrub with narrow, silvery leaves and thorny shoots, sea buckthorn bears very small yellow flowers in spring. On female plants, they are followed by small, bright orange berries in summer. They are edible and high in vitamin C.

Common name Sea buckthorn
Foliage Deciduous
Height 13–26ft (4–8m) **Spread** 13–26ft (4–8m) **Exposure** Full sun, exposed or sheltered **Soil type** Well-drained/moist but well-drained loam, sand (alkaline/neutral) **Hardiness** Zone 6

09 *Rubus idaeus*

This deciduous shrub bears tall biennial stems, some with prickles. The white flowers are followed by red, edible fruits (raspberries).

Common name Raspberry
Foliage Deciduous **Height** 5–8ft (1.5–2.5m) **Spread** 1½–3¼ft (0.5–1m) **Exposure** Full sun to full shade, exposed or sheltered **Soil** Well-drained/moist but well-drained loam, sand (acid/neutral) **Hardiness** Zones 6–7

10 *Helianthus annuus*

A fast-growing annual with large, oval to heart-shaped, hairy leaves. The flowers, up to 12in (30cm) across, have yellow petals with brownish centers. They attract bees, and the seeds that follow are food for birds.

Common name Common sunflower
Foliage Deciduous **Height** 8–13ft (2.5–4m) **Spread** 1½–3¼ft (0.5–1m) **Exposure** Sheltered, full sun **Soil** Moist but well-drained chalk, clay, loam, sand (alkaline/neutral) **Hardiness** Zones 8–9

11 *Centaurea cyanus*

Best known for the deep blue flowerheads that bloom in late spring and summer, cornflower is an upright annual with slightly lobed leaves. The flowers are edible, with a sweet/spicy clovelike flavor.

Common name Cornflower
Foliage Deciduous **Height** 1½–3¼ft (0.5–1m) **Spread** 4–20in (10–50cm) **Exposure** Full sun, exposed **Soil** Well-drained loam, sand (acid/alkaline/neutral) **Hardiness** Zones 6–7

12 *Ribes nigrum*

A deciduous self-fertile shrub producing bunches of dark purple edible berries, rich in vitamin C, in midsummer.

Common name Blackcurrant
Foliage Deciduous **Height** 3¼–5ft (1–1.5m) **Spread** 3¼–5ft (1–1.5m) **Exposure** Full sun or partial shade, sheltered **Soil** Well-drained clay, loam, sand (acid/alkaline/neutral) **Hardiness** Zones 6–7

13 *Alchemilla mollis*

This herbaceous perennial forms a clump of hairy, rounded, light green leaves. In summer, small, bright yellow flowers are borne in large sprays above the foliage. The young leaves are edible both raw and cooked; dried leaves are also used as a tea.

Common name Lady's mantle
Foliage Deciduous
Height 20–39in (50–100cm)
Spread 20–39in (50–100cm)
Exposure Full sun to full shade, exposed or sheltered **Soil** Moist but well-drained chalk, clay, loam, sand (acid/alkaline/neutral)
Hardiness Zones 6–7

14 *Trifolium pratense*

Often used as a green manure crop because it fixes nitrogen in the soil, this perennial plant has trifoliate leaves and clusters of pinkish-red flowers from midspring to early fall; both are edible. It is a great source of nectar, especially for bees.

Common name Red clover
Foliage Deciduous **Height** 4–20in (10–50cm) **Spread** 16in (40cm)
Exposure Full sun, exposed or sheltered **Soil type** Well-drained/ moist but well-drained clay, loam (acid) **Hardiness** Zone 6

15 *Fragaria vesca*

This spreading perennial forms rosettes of three-palmate, bright green leaves with toothed leaflets. In late spring, it bears white flowers that are followed by red fruit (wild strawberries) in summer.

Common name Alpine strawberry
Foliage Semievergreen **Height** 4–20in (10–50cm) **Spread** 20–39in (50–100cm) **Exposure** Full sun, sheltered **Soil type** Moist but well-drained clay, loam, sand (acid/alkaline/neutral)
Hardiness Zones 6–7

16 *Taraxacum officinale*

A herbaceous perennial with upright stems and dark green foliage. The yellow flowerheads develop into silvery tufted seedheads that disperse in the wind. It is often considered to be a weed, but all parts are used in herbal medicine or as food.

Common name Dandelion
Foliage Evergreen
Height 4–20in (10–50cm)
Spread 4–20in (10–50cm)
Exposure Full sun or partial shade, exposed or sheltered
Soil type Well-drained/moist but well-drained chalk, clay, loam, sand (acid/alkaline/neutral)
Hardiness Zone 6

17 *Matteuccia struthiopteris*

A deciduous, stoloniferous fern that forms colonies of erect rosettes, this plant has lance-shaped, bright green, bipinnatifid sterile fronds that surround shorter, brownish, fertile fronds. Young unfurled fronds are edible (but note that not all ferns are edible, so check identification before consuming).

Common name Shuttlecock fern
Foliage Deciduous **Height** 3¼–5ft (1–1.5m) **Spread** 5–8ft (1.5–2.5m)
Exposure Full shade or partial shade, sheltered **Soil** Moist but well-drained clay, loam, sand (acid/neutral)
Hardiness Zones 7–8

18 *Lonicera periclymenum*

This vigorous, twining climber has creamy-white tubular flowers 2in (5cm) long, flushed reddish-purple, that open in mid- and late summer and are very fragrant. Glossy red berries follow. Sweet nectar can be sucked from the base of plucked flowers, hence the common name.

Common name Common honeysuckle
Foliage Deciduous **Height** 13–26ft (4–8m)
Spread 8–13ft (2.5–4m) **Exposure** Full sun or partial shade, exposed or sheltered
Soil type Moist but well-drained chalk, clay, loam, sand (acid/alkaline/neutral)
Hardiness Zones 6–7

19 *Hedera helix*

A self-clinging evergreen climber, this ivy develops nonclinging branches when mature. Small, nectar-rich yellow flowers in fall are followed by black berries in winter.

Common name Common ivy **Foliage** Evergreen
Height 26–39ft (8–12m) **Spread** 8–13ft (2.5–4m)
Exposure Full sun to full shade, exposed or sheltered **Soil type** Well-drained/moist but well-drained chalk, clay, loam, sand (acid/alkaline/neutral) **Hardiness** Zones 7–8

20 Vitis vinifera

This woody plant climbs by tendrils. The leaves are three- or five-lobed and coarsely toothed. Tiny, greenish flowers bloom in summer and grapes follow in fall. The many named cultivars are selected for edible fruits or their ornamental qualities.

Common name Grape vine **Foliage** Deciduous **Height** 39ft (12m) or more **Spread** 8–13ft (2.5–4m) **Exposure** Full sun, sheltered **Soil** Well-drained chalk, loam, sand (alkaline/neutral) **Hardiness** Zones 7–8

21 Pyracantha rogersiana

A large, spiny, evergreen shrub, this has glossy oblong leaves. Its small, creamy spring flowers are followed by orange-red berries loved by birds.

Common name Asian firethorn **Foliage** Evergreen **Height** 8–13ft (2.5–4m) **Spread** 8–13ft (2.5–4m) **Exposure** Full sun or partial shade, exposed or sheltered **Soil** Well-drained chalk, clay, loam, sand (acid/alkaline/neutral) **Hardiness** Zones 7–8

Borago officinalis

This is a large, branched annual with coarsely hairy, ovate leaves. Its clusters of bright blue flowers bloom throughout summer. It can be used to make tea, and the flowers and young leaves taste like cucumber. It is also an excellent source of nectar and pollen.

Common name Borage
Foliage Deciduous
Height 20–39in (50–100cm)
Spread 4–20in (10–50cm)
Exposure Full sun or partial shade, exposed or sheltered
Soil type Well-drained chalk, clay, loam, sand (acid/alkaline/neutral)
Hardiness Zones 7–8

Actinidia arguta 'Issai'

This compact kiwi cultivar produces small, smooth fruit in late summer to early fall. Self-fertilizing, it does not need a companion in order to bear the fruit, which can be eaten "skin on."

Common name Hardy kiwi 'Issai'
Foliage Deciduous **Height** 8–13ft (2.5–4m) **Spread** 8–13ft (2.5–4m)
Exposure Full sun, sheltered
Soil Moist but well-drained clay, loam, sand (acid/alkaline)
Hardiness Zones 7–8

Passiflora caerulea

This evergreen climber with twining tendrils has dark green leaves with 5–7 fingerlike lobes. The summer flowers are white, blue, and purple and are followed by ovoid orange fruits, which are edible but not as delicious as the edible variety (*Passiflora edulis*), which is not very cold-tolerant.

Common name Blue passionflower
Foliage Semievergreen
Height up to 26ft (8m)
Spread up to 12ft (4m)
Exposure Full sun or partial shade, sheltered **Soil type** Moist but well-drained chalk, loam, sand
Hardiness Zones 8–9

Daucus carota

A tap-rooted biennial with solid, ridged stems. In summer, wild carrot bears umbels of white flowers, tinged with pink, and with a dark red central floret. The young flowers, leaves, and roots are edible—but ensure correct identification before consuming as it looks similar to poisonous hemlock (*Conium maculatum*).

Common name Wild carrot
Foliage Deciduous
Height 20–39in (50–100cm)
Spread 4–20in (10–50cm)
Exposure Full sun, exposed or sheltered **Soil type** Well-drained chalk, loam, sand (alkaline/neutral) **Hardiness** Zone 6

Jasminum officinale

A twining or scrambling evergreen shrub, this jasmine has glossy pinnate leaves and clusters of very fragrant white flowers in summer, appearing sporadically at other times. The flowers are used to flavor tea.

Common name Arabian jasmine
Foliage Evergreen
Height 8–13ft (2.5m–4m)
Spread 1¹/₂–3¹/₄ft (0.5–1m)
Exposure Partial shade, sheltered
Soil Well-drained/moist but well-drained chalk, clay, loam, sand (acid/alkaline/neutral)
Hardiness Zones 7–8

Anethum graveolens

A culinary herb with threadlike dark green leaves that have a strong, distinctive taste, dill produces umbels of small yellow flowers in summer.

Common name Dill
Foliage Deciduous
Height 20–39in (50–100cm)
Spread 4–20in (10–50cm)
Exposure Full sun, sheltered
Soil Chalk, loam, sand (acid/alkaline/neutral)
Hardiness Zones 8–9

Vicia sativa

A downy, scrambling annual with cerise flowers in a pea shape, borne singly or in pairs from spring to late summer. The seedpods are edible, resembling those of peas and beans.

Common name Common vetch
Foliage Deciduous
Height 1¹/₂–3¹/₄ft (0.5–1m)
Spread 5ft (1.5m)
Exposure Full sun, exposed or sheltered **Soil** Well-drained chalk, loam, sand (alkaline/neutral)
Hardiness Zone 6

Allium schoenoprasum

A bulbous perennial that forms a clump of erect, cylindrical leaves. The pale purple flowers bloom in summer. Both leaves and flowers are edible.

Common name Chives
Foliage Deciduous
Height 4–20in (10–50cm)
Spread 4–12in (10–30cm)
Exposure Full sun or partial shade, exposed or sheltered
Soil Well-drained/moist but well-drained chalk, clay, loam, sand (acid/alkaline/neutral)
Hardiness Zones 6–7

Phaseolus coccineus 'Tenderstar'

A twining climber with green leaves, this plant bears scarlet and pale pink flowers that develop into short, tender, runner beans. It is often grown as a summer annual.

Common name Runner bean 'Tenderstar'
Foliage Deciduous **Height** 8–13ft (2.5–4m) **Spread** 3¼–5ft (1–1.5m)
Exposure Full sun, sheltered
Soil Well-drained chalk, loam, sand (acid/alkaline/neutral)
Hardiness Zones 10–11

Achillea millefolium

This spreading stoloniferous perennial plant has narrow, finely dissected leaves. In summer, it produces small, cream or pink flat flowerheads. Both flowers and foliage add an aromatic flavor to salads and as garnishes.

Common name Common yarrow
Foliage Deciduous
Height 4–20in (10–50cm)
Spread 4–20in (10–50cm)
Exposure Full sun, exposed or sheltered **Soil** Well-drained/moist but well-drained chalk, clay, loam, sand (acid/alkaline/neutral)
Hardiness Zone 6

Filipendula ulmaria

Meadowsweet is a vigorous perennial with divided leaves and creamy-white flowers in dense terminal clusters on erect leafy stems in summer. All parts of the plant can be added to soups and stews for aromatic flavor.

Common name Meadowsweet **Foliage** Deciduous **Height** 20–39in (50–100cm) **Spread** 20–39in (50–100cm) **Exposure** Full sun or partial shade, exposed or sheltered **Soil** Moist but well-drained/poorly drained clay, loam (acid/alkaline/neutral) **Hardiness** Zones 6–7

Foeniculum vulgare

This robust, upright, aromatic biennial or short-lived perennial has pinnate leaves and flat umbels of small yellow flowers in summer. The edible leaves, flowers, and seeds add an aniseed flavor to food.

Common name Common fennel **Foliage** Deciduous **Height** 5–8ft (1.5–2.5m) **Spread** 4–20in (10–50cm) **Exposure** Full sun or partial shade, sheltered **Soil** Moist but well-drained chalk, clay, loam, sand (acid/alkaline/neutral) **Hardiness** Zones 7–8

Myrrhis odorata

An erect, aniseed-scented perennial, sweet cicely has bright green pinnate leaves and white flowers in umbels that bloom in summer, followed by spindle-shaped fruits in summer and fall.

Common name Sweet cicely **Foliage** Deciduous **Height** $3^{1}/_{4}$–5ft (1–1.5m) **Spread** $1^{1}/_{2}$–$3^{1}/_{4}$ft (0.5–1m) **Exposure** Partial shade, sheltered **Soil** Moist but well-drained loam (acid/alkaline/neutral) **Hardiness** Zones 7–8

Allium ursinum

This vigorous, bulbous perennial spreads widely, with paired, elliptic leaves and erect stems bearing umbels of starry white flowers in late spring. The leaves and flowers are edible, with a garlic taste.

Common name Ramsons **Foliage** Deciduous **Height** 4–20in (10–50cm) **Spread** 4–20in (10–50cm) **Exposure** Full sun, sheltered **Soil** Well-drained/moist but well-drained chalk, loam, sand (acid/alkaline/neutral) **Hardiness** Zone 6

Mentha requienii

A vigorous, mat-forming perennial, this plant has slender creeping and rooting stems that form extensive colonies. The bright green leaves are peppermint-scented and in summer, tubular lilac flowers are borne in short spikes. Many varieties are available with different scents.

Common name Corsican mint
Foliage Deciduous **Height** up to 4in (10cm) **Spread** Indefinite **Exposure** Full shade or partial shade, exposed or sheltered **Soil** Poorly drained/moist but well-drained clay, loam (acid/alkaline/neutral)
Hardiness Zone 6

Galium odoratum

This stoloniferous, spreading perennial forms rosettes of three-palmate, bright green leaves with toothed leaflets. In late spring, it bears cymes of white flowers that are followed by red fruit in summer. The leaves are used to add a vanilla or almond flavor to drinks.

Common name Sweet woodruff
Foliage Deciduous **Height** 4–20in (10–50cm) **Spread** 3¼–5ft (1–1.5m) **Exposure** Partial shade, sheltered **Soil** Moist but well-drained chalk, clay, loam, sand (acid/alkaline/neutral)
Hardiness Zone 6

Aronia × prunifolia

A natural hybrid between *A. arbutifolia* and *A. melanocarpa*, this shrub has a multistemmed habit. Its white flowers in late spring are followed by purple-black berries and matte, dark green leaves that turn reddish-purple colors in fall. The edible round black fruits have a slightly tart flavor.

Common name Purple chokeberry
Foliage Deciduous
Height 8–13ft (2.5–4m)
Spread 5–8ft (1.5–2.5m)
Exposure Full sun or partial shade, exposed or sheltered **Soil** Moist but well-drained clay, loam, sand (acid/neutral)
Hardiness Zone 6

Ajuga reptans

A spreading perennial, bugle forms a wide mat of dark green leaves with spikes of dark blue flowers in late spring and early summer. The young shoots can be eaten in salads or sautéed.

Common name Bugle
Foliage Evergreen
Height 4–20in (10–15cm)
Spread 20–39in (50–100cm)
Exposure Partial shade, sheltered **Soil** Moist but well–drained/poorly drained chalk, clay, loam, sand (acid/alkaline/neutral)
Hardiness Zone 6

Prunus spinosa

A small, thorny tree with dark green, ovate leaves, blackthorn produces small white flowers in early spring, followed by ovoid, bloomy black fruits in fall that are used to flavor sloe gin.

Common name Blackthorn
Foliage Deciduous
Height 8–13ft (2.5–4m)
Spread 8–13ft (2.5–4m)
Exposure Full sun, exposed or sheltered **Soil** Moist but well-drained chalk, clay, loam, sand (acid/alkaline/neutral)
Hardiness Zone 6

Rosa canina

The dog rose is a vigorous, arching shrub with midgreen foliage and pale pink or white flowers, either solitary or in small clusters, in early summer. They are followed by ovoid red fruits (rose hips) in fall that can be used to make jams and syrups.

Common name Dog rose **Foliage** Deciduous
Height 8–13ft (2.5–4m) **Spread** 5–8ft (1.5–2.5m)
Exposure Full sun, exposed or sheltered
Soil Moist but well-drained chalk, clay, loam, sand (acid/alkaline/neutral)
Hardiness Zone 6

Zanthoxylum simulans

This bushy, spiny, deciduous shrub or small tree has leaves up to 3in (8cm) long. In early summer, it bears flat-topped sprays of small, yellow-green flowers, followed by open clusters of small red fruits that split open in fall, revealing black seeds. The leaves, fruit, and bark are all aromatic, while the reddish-pink seedcases are edible and can be used as a pepper substitute.

Common name Sichuan pepper
Foliage Deciduous
Height 8–13ft (2.5–4m)
Spread 8–13ft (2.5–4m)
Exposure Full sun, sheltered
Soil type Well-drained chalk, loam, sand (acid/alkaline/neutral)
Hardiness Zones 6–7

Glycyrrhiza glabra

This vigorous herbaceous perennial has midgreen leaves up to 8in (20cm) long and pale blue to violet flowers, either solitary or in small clusters, in early summer. They are followed by coppery-red seedpods in fall. Liquorice root is commonly used as a flavoring for sweets and herbal teas.

Common name Liquorice
Foliage Deciduous
Height 3¼–5ft (1–1.5m)
Spread 1½–3¼ft (0.5–1m)
Exposure Full sun, sheltered
Soil type Moist but well-drained chalk, clay, loam, sand (acid/alkaline/neutral)
Hardiness Zones 7–8

Cydonia oblonga

Quince is a dense large shrub or small tree with oval, midgreen leaves. The pale pink to white late spring flowers are followed by edible, golden-yellow, pear-shaped fruit in fall.

Common name Quince **Foliage** Deciduous **Height** 8–13ft (2.5m–4m) **Spread** 8–13ft (2.5m–4m) **Exposure** Full sun, sheltered **Soil** Moist but well-drained clay, loam (acid/alkaline/neutral) **Hardiness** Zones 7–8

Mespilus germanica

This small tree or large shrub has oblong leaves turning yellow-brown in fall. White flowers in late spring are followed by brown fruit in fall, used to make medlar jelly.

Common name Common medlar **Foliage** Deciduous **Height** 13–26ft (4–8m) **Spread** 13–26ft (4–8m) **Exposure** Full sun or partial shade, exposed or sheltered **Soil** Well-drained/moist but well-drained chalk, clay, loam, sand (acid/alkaline/neutral) **Hardiness** Zones 6–7

Corylus avellana

This large, spreading deciduous shrub or small tree has yellow male catkins in early spring followed by edible nuts in fall, when the rounded leaves turn yellow before falling.

Common name Hazel **Foliage** Deciduous **Height** 13–26ft (4–8m) **Spread** 13–26ft (4–8m) **Exposure** Full sun or partial shade, exposed or sheltered **Soil** Well-drained/moist but well-drained chalk, loam, sand (alkaline/neutral) **Hardiness** Zones 6–7

Crataegus monogyna

A small, rounded deciduous tree, this has glossy, lobed leaves and flat sprays of cream flowers in spring, followed in fall by dark red berries. Its nickname of "bread and cheese" refers to the fresh growth of leaves (the bread) and the spring buds (the cheese), both of which are edible.

Common name Common hawthorn
Foliage Deciduous **Height** 13–26ft (4–8m)
Spread 13–26ft (4–8m) **Exposure** Full sun or partial shade, exposed or sheltered
Soil Well-drained/moist but well-drained chalk, clay, loam, sand (acid/alkaline/neutral)
Hardiness Zone 6

Vaccinium myrtillus

This deciduous, suckering, usually prostrate shrub has dense, bright green stems and ovate, glossy leaves, often flushed red in fall. The pink flowers in late spring to early summer are followed by blue-black, edible berries in fall.

Common name Common bilberry
Foliage Deciduous **Height** 4–20in (10–50cm) **Spread** 20–39in (50–100cm) **Exposure** Full sun or partial shade, exposed or sheltered
Soil Well-drained/moist but well-drained loam, sand (acid)
Hardiness Zones 6–7

MARTIN CRAWFORD has spent more than 30 years in organic agriculture and horticulture and is the founder of the Agroforestry Research Trust. His Forest Garden Project incorporates diverse trees, shrubs, and ground cover, all contributing to a self-sustaining ecosystem with edible and medicinal produce.

Martin's forest garden in Devon is dense and complex, with a rich tapestry of productive plants designed to emulate a natural forest.

"

DESIGNING A FOREST GARDEN CAN BE OVERWHELMING. DO YOU HAVE ANY TIPS FOR GETTING STARTED?

Good forest garden design aims to maximize diversity, often with 200 or more species, but this could be far less in small spaces. This level of complexity can appear overwhelming, but generally, designing from the top down works well: plant the canopy (tree) layer first; next the shrub layer; and finally the ground layer. This process is often spread over 3–10 years, which means that shade starts to develop, so shade-loving plants can be introduced in the understory planting.

HAVE YOU SEEN ANY CLIMATE-INDUCED CHANGES INFLUENCING WHAT YOU CAN GROW SINCE YOU HAVE BEEN EXPERIMENTING WITH FOREST GARDENS IN DEVON?

Medlar fruits ripen on trees now, and persimmons ripen in Devon increasingly frequently; some formerly herbaceous plants are becoming evergreen. Some of the changes are negative, such as Devon varieties of apples doing increasingly poorly.

One of our projects is a subtropical "forest garden greenhouse" using a novel ground-heat storage system for winter heating; it has a climate 9°F (5°C) warmer than outside (moving Devon to SW Portugal). In here, we're experimenting with crops, some of which will become more viable outside as our climate warms.

YOUR FOREST GARDENS HAVE A STAGGERING AMOUNT OF BIODIVERSITY IN THE PLANTING. HAVE YOU COMPARED THEM WITH NATIVE WOODLAND?

Two studies have compared the invertebrate diversity of the Dartington forest garden with native woodland. In one, a comparison with a reforested site showed that the forest garden hosts not only a more diverse but also a more even and abundant community of invertebrates than the reforested site.

In a comparison with another native woodland site, the forest garden was seen to support a more robust and varied population of invertebrates. These results show that diversity can be at least as important to wildlife as native species.

199

GREEN ROOF PLANTING

01

THE PLANTINGS USED FOR A GREEN ROOF ARE OFTEN PREGROWN IN A MAT OR TRAY. THERE ARE A NUMBER OF PRODUCTS AVAILABLE OFF THE SHELF, MANY OF WHICH CONTAIN A MIX OF SEDUM SPECIES, OR YOU CAN USE CONTAINERIZED OR BARE-ROOT INDIVIDUAL PLANTS.

The depth of the soil on a green roof is important, as it dictates the type of plants that will succeed. The plants suggested here are based on a shallow substrate depth of 1½–2½in (4–6cm). This depth is referred to as an extensive green roof (see p.108). If your roof structure can take a greater substrate depth, then the choice of plants increases dramatically. If, for example, you have 4in (10cm) of soil, many planted pathway species that are drought-resilient could be sustained. If you have deeper soil still, such as 8in (20cm), then many of the drought-resilient gravel garden plants would also be sustainable on the green roof. At this depth, the roof is referred to as semiextensive. A depth of 12–20in (30–50cm) would enable a huge range of perennials and shrubs to be grown, but at these depths, the green roof weight gets very heavy. Trees can generally be grown in soil depths of 2½–4½ft (80–130cm).

SEDUM

Sedum species are ubiquitous in green roof plantings, as they are well suited to a hot, exposed, and arid site; these are the conditions in which they grow naturally. Their fleshy, succulent leaves are designed to store water and have a thick, waxy surface with the ability to close its pores rather than lose water through respiration.

01 *Chamaemelum nobile*

This mat-forming perennial has finely divided, aromatic leaves and white daisy flowers with yellow centers, ½in (1.5cm) across. The dried flowers of the plant can be used to make a relaxing herbal tea.

Common name Common chamomile
Foliage Deciduous
Height 4–20in (10–50cm)
Spread 4–20in (10–50cm)
Exposure Full sun or partial shade, exposed or sheltered
Soil Well-drained chalk, loam, sand (acid/alkaline/neutral)
Hardiness Zone 6

02 *Phedimus spurius*

A vigorous, mat-forming, semievergreen perennial, this plant has fleshy, toothed leaves that are held on spreading, rooting stems. In late summer, star-shaped, pink or white flowers are borne in clusters.

Common name Caucasian stonecrop **Foliage** Semievergreen **Height** 4in (10cm)
Spread 4–20in (10–50cm)
Exposure Full sun, sheltered
Soil Well-drained/moist but well-drained chalk, loam, sand (alkaline/neutral)
Hardiness Zones 7–8

03 *Sedum reflexum*

A fast-growing, mat-forming perennial, this sedum has succulent, pointed, cylindrical leaves. In summer, stems up to 6in (15cm) tall bear clusters of star-shaped yellow flowers that are pendent in bud but turn upward as they open.

Common name Cock's comb stonecrop **Foliage** Evergreen
Height 4–20in (10–50cm)
Spread 4–20in (10–50cm)
Exposure Full sun, sheltered
Soil Well-drained chalk, loam, sand (alkaline/neutral)
Hardiness Zones 7–8

Sedum acre

This mat-forming, hairless, succulent perennial has small, ovoid, fleshy leaves close to the stems. Yellow, star-shaped flowers bloom in spring and summer.

Common name Biting stonecrop
Foliage Evergreen
Height 4in (10cm)
Spread 4in (10cm)
Exposure Full sun, exposed or sheltered **Soil** Well-drained or moist but well-drained chalk, loam, sand (acid/alkaline/neutral)
Hardiness Zone 6

Sempervivum montanum

A vigorous, mat-forming, evergreen succulent with rosettes of sharp-pointed, fleshy, finely hairy leaves. Short, leafy stems bear reddish-purple flowers in summer.

Common name Mountain houseleek
Foliage Evergreen **Height** 4in (10cm)
Spread 12in (30cm) **Exposure** Full sun, exposed or sheltered **Soil** Well-drained loam, sand (acid/alkaline/neutral)
Hardiness Zones 8–9

Sedum kamtschaticum

This low, clump-forming, semievergreen perennial has bright green leaves, accompanied in late summer by golden-yellow flowers with finely pointed petals.

Common name Orange stonecrop
Foliage Semievergreen **Height** 4in (10cm)
Spread 4–20in (10–50cm) **Exposure** Full sun, exposed or sheltered **Soil** Well-drained chalk, loam, sand (alkaline/neutral)
Hardiness Zones 7–8

Sedum kamtschaticum var. *floriferum* 'Weihenstephaner Gold'

This variety forms a low, spreading clump of spoon-shaped leaves tinged with bronze. In late summer, it bears starry pale yellow flowers that take on a tinge of pink.

Common name Orange stonecrop 'Weihenstephaner Gold'
Foliage Semievergreen
Height 4in (10cm) **Spread** 4–20in (10–50cm) **Exposure** Full sun or partial shade, exposed
Soil type Well-drained chalk, loam, sand (alkaline/neutral)
Hardiness Zones 7–8

Sedum album 'Coral Carpet'

This evergreen, mat-forming perennial has small, succulent, rounded green leaves that are flushed with red. Clusters of starry white flowers bloom in early summer.

Common name Coral carpet
Foliage Evergreen
Height 4in (10cm)
Spread 4in (10cm)
Exposure Full sun, sheltered
Soil type Well-drained loam, sand (acid/alkaline/neutral)
Hardiness Zone 6

Sempervivum arachnoideum

This evergreen perennial forms a mat of fleshy rosettes of green or reddish leaves with cobwebby white hairs at the tips. It bears starry pink flowers in summer.

Common name Cobweb houseleek
Foliage Evergreen **Height** 4in (10cm) **Spread** 4–20in (10–50cm) **Exposure** Full sun, exposed or sheltered **Soil type** Loam, sand (acid/alkaline/neutral)
Hardiness Zone 6

Sempervivum tectorum

A vigorous mat-forming perennial, this plant has clusters of fleshy rosettes up to 4in (10cm) across, the blue-green leaves suffused with reddish-purple. Purplish-pink flowers with narrow pointed petals are borne on stems up to 8in (20cm) tall.

Common name Common houseleek
Foliage Evergreen **Height** 4in (10cm)
Spread 4–20in (10–50cm) **Exposure** Full sun, exposed or sheltered **Soil type** Well-drained loam, sand (acid/alkaline/neutral)
Hardiness Zone 6

CHAPTER SIX

SUSTAINABLE MATERIALS

For this project by Peter and Anneliese Latz, a steelworks has been transformed into a landscape park. A unique design approach led to the buildings being recycled rather than torn down. Blast furnaces are used as follies, concrete tanks as walled gardens, and water tanks as water gardens. Instead of importing new soils, if an industrial process left an unusual soil mixture, plants that could tolerate the substrate were chosen.

SUSTAINABLE MATERIALS

HARD MATERIALS ARE IMPORTANT TO ALLOW US TO MOVE THROUGH A LANDSCAPE, AS WELL AS TO PROVIDE A STABLE SURFACE FOR ELEMENTS SUCH AS DINING TABLES AND SEATING. THIS CHAPTER EXPLORES WHERE COMMON BUILDING MATERIALS COME FROM AND HOW SUSTAINABLE THEY ARE.

As urban sprawl increases across the globe, we need to view our gardens as part of the wider landscape. From the outset, we need to consider the carbon footprint of the hard landscaping we plan to install. How much carbon would it cost to remove it? Is it biodegradable, or does it contain plastic, concrete, or other materials that will take hundreds or thousands of years to break down? How far will the materials travel from supplier to the garden, and how many suppliers are they coming from? Sourcing locally or from fewer suppliers could drastically reduce the carbon footprint of a hard-landscaping scheme.

CONSIDER MAINTENANCE

Certain materials require a lot of maintenance, such as a painted wall or fence; unless you accept the aesthetic of the weathered paint, you will need to repaint periodically to keep it looking fresh. In contrast, materials such as natural stone or weathering steel (which develops a layer of rust that protects the steel beneath) need little or no maintenance, and they harmonize with their environment as they age, improving their aesthetic.

WASTE MATERIALS

The construction industry produces huge amounts of waste, but waste materials have their own aesthetic and can be made beautiful. Reclaimed timber, for example, has a patina of age, character, and texture that cannot be imitated. The same is true of natural reclaimed stone rather than an imitation product such as precast cement. The age, character, and unique aesthetic of every slab gives each piece an inherent beauty.

DURABLE VS. SUSTAINABLE

Durability is often seen as an important factor in the choice of materials: concrete, stone, and other heavy materials will have a long lifespan if installed correctly. However, if this is in a sensitive landscape or in a dwelling that won't be occupied long-term by the current residents, the lifespan is irrelevant. It is common to see gardens that were built to last 100 years being replaced because fashions or requirements have changed. So durability is only sustainable if the long-term installation of the scheme is ensured. Otherwise, a more sustainable choice would be low-impact, biodegradable materials that are easy to remove or recycle, such as timber.

EMBODIED CARBON

PUT SIMPLY, EMBODIED CARBON IS THE CARBON FOOTPRINT OF A LANDSCAPING OR BUILDING PROJECT. IT REFERS TO THE CARBON DIOXIDE (CO_2) EMISSIONS ASSOCIATED WITH THE MATERIALS AND CONSTRUCTION PROCESSES THROUGHOUT THE LIFECYCLE OF A PROJECT.

Embodied carbon refers to the CO_2 that is produced by maintaining and eventually demolishing the project, transporting the waste, and recycling it. It can be measured in three ways: from cradle to (factory) gate, from cradle to site (of use), or from cradle to grave (end of life).

HOW TO REDUCE THE EMBODIED CARBON OF YOUR PROJECT

- Limit the use of high-carbon materials such as cement, metal, and plastic. Wood is becoming increasingly popular as a building material due to its lower embodied carbon levels and, if produced sustainably, carbon storage potential.
- Limit new materials: construction processes have a high carbon footprint. Reclaiming, renovating, reusing, or repurposing existing materials can greatly reduce a project's embodied carbon levels.
- Use recycled materials where possible, especially those with high levels of embodied carbon such as metal and plastic. This saves on the amount of carbon being emitted to produce new materials.
- Source materials locally instead of shipping from overseas to reduce emissions associated with transportation. Research where the materials you want to use come from and aim to source from as close as possible to the site.
- Consider complexity: if your project is easy and quick to construct, it is likely that less carbon will be emitted from the construction process.

THE COMPLEXITY OF CARBON DATA

Embodied carbon data is constantly evolving as manufacturing processes develop and are updated; the information on the graph opposite is from the University of Bath Inventory of Carbon and Energy (ICE) Database V3, 2019. Also, manufacturing processes vary globally and embodied carbon levels associated with materials will fluctuate from one region to another. The calculations are complex, too. For smaller residential projects, this level of data calculation may be impractical, but an understanding of emissions involved in the production of materials can still inform sustainable material choices.

LIFECYCLE

This flow chart shows approximate distribution of emissions in the lifecycle of a material: 50 percent of the embodied carbon is produced in manufacturing the product; 5 percent in the construction; 43 percent in the lifecycle; and 2 percent at the end of its life.

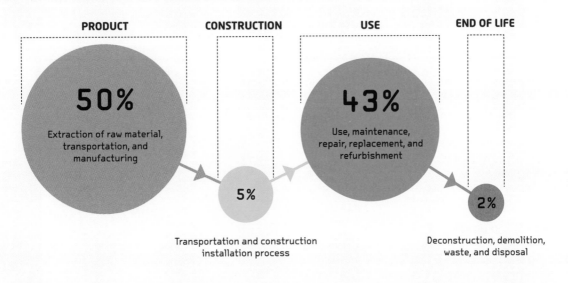

PRODUCT

50%

Extraction of raw material, transportation, and manufacturing

CONSTRUCTION

5%

Transportation and construction installation process

USE

43%

Use, maintenance, repair, replacement, and refurbishment

END OF LIFE

2%

Deconstruction, demolition, waste, and disposal

EMBODIED CARBON

This graph shows embodied carbon from source to manufacturing for a number of common landscaping materials. The graph illustrates the amount of carbon used to produce each material but doesn't account for carbon emissions in shipping or installation on site, as these will vary greatly depending on where and how they are being installed. The carbon stored in timber means it can have a negative value, essentially reducing the embodied carbon of a project. However, carbon storage can only be claimed for sustainably sourced timber.

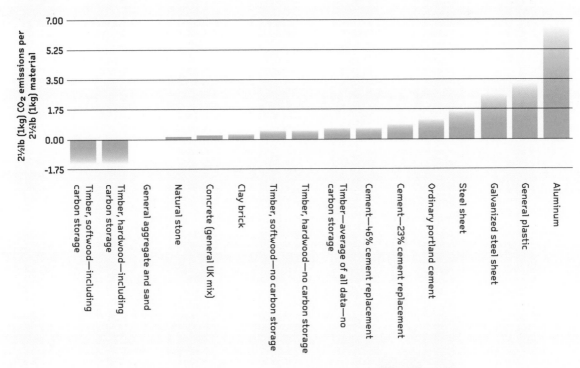

HARDWOOD AND SOFTWOOD

Generally, hardwood comes from slower-growing deciduous trees that shed their leaves every year: the slow rate of growth causes the timber to be denser and harder. Softwood is derived from faster-growing coniferous trees, which usually remain evergreen; the faster growth rate means the timber is less dense. Hardwoods have a longer lifespan, as their density means they are more resilient to weathering.

However, both softwoods and hardwoods can be treated to extend lifespan. Treatments often require regular application, so they need to be factored into the maintenance regime. Also, access needs to be considered: a stained fence covered in climbing plants will be difficult to restain unless all of the plants are removed. Leaving timber to weather naturally is often the most sustainable and low-maintenance option.

WEATHERED WOOD

Timber changes color due to lignin being degraded by the UV light present in natural sunlight. The degraded lignin is then washed out of the wood by rainfall and ambient moisture in the air. The remaining fibers on the wood surface are more resistant to leaching and UV degradation and contain high levels of cellulose, which is white/gray, giving weathered timber its silvery color.

RECLAIMED TIMBER

High-quality reclaimed timber is available from reclamation yards. It may need processing, such as sanding, but as it is a recycled product, the carbon footprint is lower—particularly compared to virgin tropical hardwood timber, which is often removed from a sensitive habitat and shipped long distances. If reclaimed timber is difficult to source, sustainable softwood timber products also exist as good low-carbon alternatives.

TIMBER

TIMBER IS WOOD PREPARED FOR BUILDING, LANDSCAPING, OR CARPENTRY, WITH DIFFERING CHARACTERISTICS, SUCH AS GRAIN, DENSITY, COLOR, AND HARDNESS. MANY SPECIES OF TREE ARE SUITABLE FOR USE AS TIMBER, BUT THEY MAY ALSO BE UNDER THREAT FROM ILLEGAL LOGGING, CAUSING DEFORESTATION IN HIGHLY SENSITIVE ENVIRONMENTS.

[Top] The trees native to the Konkan western coastline forest in Maharastra, India, are prey to illegal deforestation. Logging operations need careful and considered management to ensure that resources are not depleted faster than they are regrown.
[Left] A path through lush vegetation in Costa Rica, Central America, where conservation efforts are in place to protect local species.

TEAK

Tectona grandis
When teak trees are grown in sustainably managed forests, the carbon sequestration and the potential for diverse land use means using teak can be sustainable—but illegal logging diminishes habitats.

Slow-growing hardwood

Origin South and Southeast Asia. Myanmar's teak forest makes up almost half the world's naturally growing teak.

Shipping From Asia, shipping distances for use in Europe and the US are considerable.

Lifespan Hard and durable; resistant to termite, fungus, and weathering; it has a long lifespan and the potential to be recycled for bioenergy.

YELLOW BALAU

Shorea laevis
Yellow balau can have a fairly low carbon footprint when the waste is used to make byproducts, offsetting emissions produced during processing. But it is considered vulnerable: it is logged for timber and deforested for agriculture.

Tropical hardwood

Origin Native to Myanmar, Thailand, Sumatra, Peninsular Malaysia, and Borneo.

Shipping Long travel distances between tropical regions and Europe and the US.

Lifespan Durable and resistant to rot. The wood can be reused or burned as bioenergy.

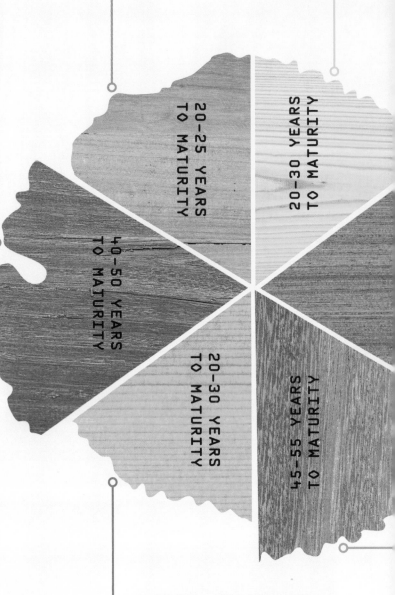

20–25 YEARS TO MATURITY

20–30 YEARS TO MATURITY

40–50 YEARS TO MATURITY

20–30 YEARS TO MATURITY

45–55 YEARS TO MATURITY

TYPES OF TIMBER

THE TYPES OF TIMBER COMPARED HERE ARE COMMONLY USED FOR LANDSCAPING AND GARDENING PROJECTS. THERE ARE SEVERAL THINGS TO BEAR IN MIND WHEN MAKING SUSTAINABLE CHOICES.

WESTERN RED CEDAR

Thuja plicata
Western red cedar is considered fast-growing, and the durable wood is good for construction.

Fast-growing softwood

Origin Western North America; naturalized in the UK and assimilated into other temperate zones, such as Western Europe, Australia, and New Zealand.

Shipping Carbon impact is low when sourced from sustainable local forests.

Lifespan Possesses a natural preservative that makes it resistant to fungal attack. Cedar cladding can last for 40–60 years.

SIBERIAN LARCH

Larix sibirica
Siberian larch is being replanted faster than it is being harvested, making this a very sustainable choice. Its resistance to rot when in contact with the ground makes it suitable for fence posts.

Softwood

Origin Northern hemisphere; the European larch (*Larix decidua*) is native to the mountains of Central Europe.

Shipping Carbon impact is low when sourced from sustainable local forests.

Lifespan Moderately durable and resistant to rot; does not require preservatives to sustain its longevity.

100–120 YEARS TO MATURITY

EUROPEAN OAK

Quercus robur
Manufacturing oak can be sustainable, as a lot of the energy required can be produced from burning wood waste. Oak is a common tree species and often grown for harvesting. If forests are well managed, then this can be a sustainable choice.

Slow-growing hardwood

Origin Northern hemisphere.

Shipping Carbon impact is low when sourced from sustainable local forests.

Lifespan Durable, long-lasting, and can be reused and recycled.

IROKO

Milicia excelsa
Illegal logging has jeopardized iroko in many areas. It is classified as "at risk" due to a reduction of more than 20 percent over the past 75 years, caused by a dwindling of its natural span and exploitation.

Tropical hardwood

Origin Native to the west coast of Africa.

Shipping For use in the US and Europe, the carbon impact of shipping should be considered for a resilient garden.

Lifespan Iroko is very durable and is resistant to rot and insect assault.

GARDEN DURABILITY
Several factors will affect how long timber lasts in your garden, such as atmospheric moisture, installation quality, and local insects. This graph ranks the durability of popular types of timber when installed above ground.
1: 25 years or more, 2: 15–25 years, 3: 10–15 years.

Teak	1
Yellow balau	2
Western red cedar	3
Iroko	2
European oak	2
Siberian larch	3

CARBON STORING CAPACITY
The natural forest environments these species grow in have huge capacity to store carbon and need sensitive management to keep the carbon out of the atmosphere. This graph represents carbon stored per hectare of the natural environments these species are found in.

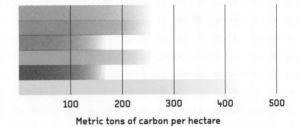

100   200   300   400   500

Metric tons of carbon per hectare

COMMON USES
Each type of timber can be used in multiple ways in the garden. Hardwood types tend to last longer.

Fencing			●	●	● ●
Furniture	●			●	●
Cladding			●	●	● ●
Decking		●	●	●	●

NATURAL STONE

NATURAL STONE AND OTHER MINERAL-BASED PRODUCTS ARE OFTEN USED IN GARDEN LANDSCAPING, POPULAR FOR THEIR APPEARANCE AND LONGEVITY. AS STONE IS HEAVY, THE CARBON FOOTPRINT IS HIGH WHEN IT IS SHIPPED OVER LONG DISTANCES.

Natural stone indicates organic rock quarried directly from the Earth. It is durable and can stand up to varying weather conditions and fluctuating temperatures. This makes it an environmentally green choice in terms of longevity, and it can be crushed up and used as aggregate when it is no longer in good condition. However, where it comes from is pertinent in terms of proximity to the site, as long-distance transport of a high-weight product can command a high carbon footprint.

ROCK TYPES

Igneous rocks form when magma or lava (molten rock) from beneath the Earth's crust cools and then solidifies. They often have visible large crystals and are extremely hard.
Examples: basalt, gabbro, granite.

Metamorphic rocks originate when igneous, sedimentary, or existing metamorphic rocks are changed via environmental factors such as heat or pressure.
Examples: marble, quartzite, slate.

Sedimentary rocks form on or near the surface of the Earth. They result from rock erosion that produces sedimentary material such as sand and mud, which is then compressed into new layers of rock.
Examples: chalk, limestone, sandstone.

[Left] Heavy-duty machinery is used to extract and cut natural stone, which can be damaging to the environment. However, stone is a natural material and requires little additional processing, so embodied carbon in its manufacture is relatively low in comparison to some heavily processed materials.

[Below] Quarrying for stone can scar the natural landscape and damage habitat, but disused quarries can become biodiversity hotspots, the diverse topography providing habitat for plants and invertebrates.

TYPES OF STONE

HERE ARE SOME OF THE MANY TYPES OF NATURAL STONE AND STONE-BASED PRODUCTS, SUCH AS PORCELAIN, THAT CAN BE USED FOR PATHS, WALKWAYS, SEATING AREAS, RETAINING WALLS, WATER FEATURES, CLADDING, AND SCULPTURES.

BRAZILIAN SLATE

Slate extracted from Brazil is regarded as a high-quality natural stone. It only requires low-intensity production after extraction, but shipping it long distances can be carbon intensive.

Origin 95 percent of Brazilian slate is a metamorphic rock extracted from the Minas Gerais region, about 280 miles (450km) north of Rio de Janeiro.

Lifespan Natural slate can withstand fluctuating conditions such as temperature and moisture. Strong and hard-wearing, it can endure for centuries, hence its use for roofing tiles. It can be recycled into chippings.

YORKSTONE

This sandstone is extracted from quarries in Yorkshire, UK, using heavy machinery. It requires little processing after extraction and no toxic chemicals are used in production. It has a relatively low carbon footprint.

Origin Sedimentary rock quarries in Yorkshire, UK.

Lifespan Yorkstone was used historically in the UK for paving in market towns with a lot of human traffic and horses and carts. A popular choice for its strength and durability, it is very resistant to damage and can serve a useable lifespan of more than than 100 years.

PORCELAIN

Porcelain tiles are made by mixing natural clay with feldspar (a group of rock-forming aluminum tectosilicate minerals), quartz, water, and pigment, then baking it in a kiln at very high temperatures. The tiles can be produced with recycled elements, but the manufacturing process is more intensive than that for natural stone, resulting in a higher carbon footprint.

Origin Porcelain tiles are processed on an industrial scale in many countries globally.

Lifespan Baking at high temperatures makes porcelain tiles very hard-wearing, and they can sustain a lot of human traffic. They are viewed as very long-lasting, but the thickness and quality of the tiles can vary from different suppliers, so be wary of low-cost options.

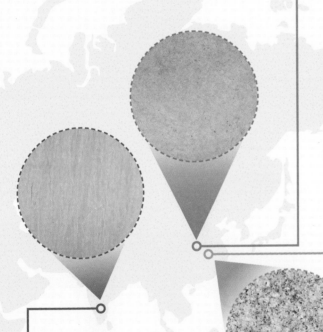

CHINESE GRANITE

Like all natural stone, granite is extracted with heavy machinery and requires little processing. Granite from China tends to be cheaper than European granite, but can have ethical drawbacks, with some supply chains being linked to slavery and child labor.

Origin An igneous rock, quarried in China.

Lifespan Granite is incredibly hard-wearing and long-lasting when it is correctly installed, with a potential lifespan of about 100 years.

INDIAN SANDSTONE

Indian sandstone is usually extracted from the ground by placing explosives at fault lines. Ethical credentials vary; look for importers who are signed up to the Ethical Trade Initiative.

Origin A sedimentary rock quarried in India.

Lifespan Indian sandstone is softer and less durable than harder and denser types of stone, and is therefore generally cheaper. When it is correctly installed, Indian sandstone paving has a lifespan of about 30–50 years or more, so it is still considered a durable material.

GRAVEL

GRAVEL REFERS TO A MIX OF COARSE ROCK OR MINERAL FRAGMENTS: ANYTHING LARGER THAN 0.2 IN (4 MM) AND UP TO ABOUT 3 IN (76 MM).

01

Gravel is used for many purposes, including subbase and drainage, driveways, and decorative mulches. Laid on a permeable subbase, it allows water to permeate to the ground below.

Aggregates for gravel are sourced from quarries or strip-mined from the seabed at many locations worldwide. Examples are pea shingle, granite, and limestone. Many countries around the world have sources of aggregate for gravel, but these take a lot

03

[01] Beth Chatto's famous gravel garden in Essex, a dry part of the UK. The gravel is used as a mulch to improve the drought resilience of the planting scheme. [02] Harbor dredging near Venice, Italy, where material is ripped from the seabed, which can damage the marine environment. [03] Prospect Cottage was the home of British filmmaker Derek Jarman, located on a shingle beach. The harsh environment supports only the most rugged plants.

of resources to extract, which can cause damage to the environment; when materials for gravel are dredged from the seabed, this can disturb marine life and destroy habitats. Recycled aggregate is usually a repurposed waste product such as washed and graded demolition rubble, crushed concrete or ceramics, or reclaimed stone.

When gravel is transported from afar, its weight can command a large carbon footprint, but locally sourced gravel is an option in many countries. Recycled aggregate is often handled close to the construction site and can be found locally to many sites. Reusing material also circumvents the demand for landfill disposal, along with all the associated transport and environmental repercussions.

With appropriate installation and maintenance, a gravel driveway can last for more than 100 years, with the benefit that it is easy to refill with more material if needed.

RECYCLED GRAVEL

In 2020, recycled and secondary sources of aggregates accounted for 28 percent (69.2 million tons/61.8 million metric tons) of total aggregates supply in the UK, a leading position internationally in the use of these materials.

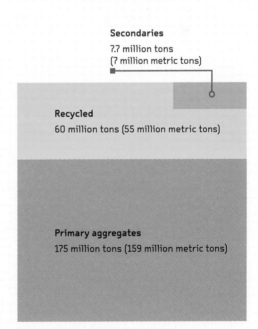

Secondaries
7.7 million tons
(7 million metric tons)

Recycled
60 million tons (55 million metric tons)

Primary aggregates
175 million tons (159 million metric tons)

221

China is the biggest manufacturer of cement; it is estimated to have produced 2.8 billion tons (2.5 billion metric tons) in 2021, approximately half of the world's cement. Concrete is the most used building material in the world, and second only to water as a resource used globally.

CEMENT

Cement is used to bind materials together in the form of mortar, which is composed from a mixture of a fine aggregate (typically sand), cement, and water. It is used as a bedding later for paving, or to bond bricks together in a wall.

CONCRETE

An amalgamation of aggregate fused together with cement, usually activated by water, concrete hardens as it cures. As concrete is very durable and able to stand up to extreme weather, it is used to make furniture, sculptural elements, and paving. It is thought that concrete uses nearly 10 percent of global industrial water consumption and accounts for 4–8 percent of carbon dioxide emissions globally—coal, oil, and gas are the only substances emitting higher levels of greenhouse gas. The production of clinker (nodules of limestone and clay heated to high temperatures in a kiln) is the most energy-exhaustive stage of manufacturing cement, and this is thought to account for 50 percent of concrete's carbon dioxide emissions.

CEMENT AND CONCRETE

CEMENT IS USED TO BIND MATERIALS TOGETHER AS IT SETS. IN CONSTRUCTION, IT IS USUALLY INORGANIC MATTER WITH A LIME OR CALCIUM SILICATE BASE. WHEN COMBINED WITH WATER, SAND, AND AGGREGATES, CEMENT PRODUCES CONCRETE.

Concrete buildings are expected to last for at least 100 years if sufficiently maintained. In areas with increased exposure to wear and tear, such as pavements, concrete is anticipated to have a lifespan of about 50 years.

CEMENT PRODUCTION

Cement production emits a lot of carbon dioxide. This graphic shows that producing 1 ton of conventional cement in Australia emits about 0.82 metric tons of carbon dioxide.

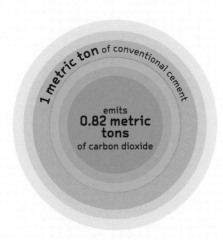

1 metric ton of conventional cement

emits
0.82 metric tons
of carbon dioxide

GROWING EMISSIONS

This graph shows global carbon dioxide emissions from rising cement production over the past century. There isn't an easy way of reducing the emissions from cement production, but a move toward alternative products will help reduce global emissions.

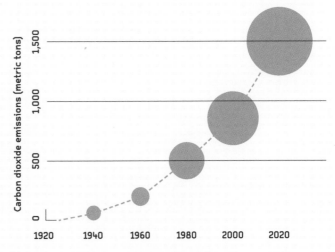

Carbon dioxide emissions (metric tons)

1,500 — 1,000 — 500 — 0

1920 1940 1960 1980 2000 2020

CONCRETE ALTERNATIVES

CONCRETE IS USED WIDELY IN GARDEN LANDSCAPING, FROM FOUNDATIONS TO SURFACE PAVING, BUT THERE ARE SOME ALTERNATIVES THAT CAN DO THE SAME JOB WITH A REDUCED CARBON FOOTPRINT.

GREEN CONCRETE

One of the best ways to move toward an eco-friendly construction material rather than using traditional concrete is to fully or partly replace energy-intensive cement with recycled or waste materials. Fly ash (waste from burning coal), silica fume (a superfine dust, a byproduct of silicon and ferrosilicon alloy production), and wood ash are some examples. By making use of the byproducts and waste from various manufacturing sectors, concrete needs less energy to produce and also eases the pressure on natural resources. Not only does it cause lower carbon dioxide emissions, it is also thought of as being less costly and can be even more durable than conventional concrete. Reducing water consumption by reusing wash water is among the many tactics employed to accomplish more sustainable concrete production.

Green concrete is defined as concrete that uses waste materials as at least one element of its material composition, and/or the manufacturing process isn't environmentally damaging, and/or it has a sustainable life cycle, for example, long durability. It can have a low carbon footprint if based on reused water and locally sourced waste materials and aggregates. Considered extremely durable, it has a high tensile strength and is resistant to corrosion. A slower rate of shrinkage can mean it is more long-lasting than traditional concrete.

RAMMED EARTH

Rammed earth is an ancient building technique, with evidence of its use dating back to the Neolithic period. Materials such as dampened subsoil, clay, and aggregates are compressed in layers between a temporary timber structure known as formwork that is removed once the rammed earth has dried out. Robust, naturally insulating, and environmentally friendly, it also provides a striking, earthy aesthetic.

The materials can be found on or close to site, so transport emissions are low. Rammed earth has a carbon footprint around 40 times lower than concrete. It is also entirely recyclable and nontoxic.

TERRAZZO

A composite material, terrazzo is traditionally made from waste marble chippings set into cement or, for internal use, resin. It is either formed and poured by hand or precast into large blocks that are then sawn to size. Terrazzo can be set in a green cement binder and a range of waste materials used in place of marble—for example, wood chips, rubble, or even scrap metal or plastic. The waste materials take on a new aesthetic when polished smooth, with the individual elements providing a mosaic texture. Waste material, particularly construction waste, is abundant across the globe, so using it creatively is a sustainable practice to keep it from going to landfills.

COB

Cob comprises straw, sand, earth, and clay combined with water. Lime is also sometimes a component. It can be molded into versatile forms, and the technique results in a long-lasting and sturdy structure. Cob-work has been used for centuries, with some ancient structures surviving to this day. It has become a popular sustainable choice for construction.

[01] A desire to create a locally sourced and sustainable paving material led me to collaborate with Diespeker & Co. in London to produce a terrazzolike material using rubble and waste materials—the name Rubblazzo reflects the mixture of rubble and terrazzo. When set in green concrete and polished back, the rubble takes on a new aesthetic, with the individual elements—crushed concrete, brick, ceramic, or glass—providing a mosaic texture.

02

NATURAL RESOURCES

By making use of the byproducts and waste from various manufacturing sectors, green concrete uses less energy to produce than conventional concrete and also eases the pressure on natural resources.

03

[02] Rammed earth walls were a stunning feature on Sarah Price's 2018 show garden at the RHS Chelsea Flower Show.
[03] Cob has been used for centuries in construction and is highly sustainable, especially when made with materials from the site. It sits beautifully here alongside local stone.

Using 350 cu ft (10 cu m) of green concrete saves 2.8 metric tons of carbon dioxide—the equivalent of planting 14 trees.

PLASTIC

PLASTICS ARE A BROAD RANGE OF MATERIALS THAT ARE SYNTHETIC OR SEMISYNTHETIC, USING POLYMERS AS A CHIEF COMPONENT. WHILE MANY CAN BE RECYCLED, MOST TAKE THOUSANDS OF YEARS TO BREAK DOWN.

Plastic is versatile, lightweight, generally low-cost, and widely used in most gardens. Compost and tools come wrapped in it; plants are sold in plastic pots; and it is used for hoses, weed barriers, spray bottles—the list of products is extensive. While some plastics are recyclable, and there is a range of recycled plastic products available—including decking, furniture, and pots—where possible, try to use alternative materials in the garden that are less environmentally damaging.

Ocean plastic waste is a common sight across the globe, from busy city beaches to remote islands. Here, a boy in Manila, in the Philippines, collects plastic waste for recycling on the beach.

RECYCLING PLASTIC

The recycling logo on plastics shows numbers that are resin identification codes, which helps recycling plants sort materials. The numbers 1-7 inform workers what kind of plastic it is and how it should be processed.

PETE OR PET

Used for most clear plastic bottles.

Full name Polyethylene terephthalate

Origin Crude oil and natural gas are used to extract the raw materials to make PET plastic.

Lifespan PET bottles can be reused, including as cloches to cover seedlings. While PET is not biodegradable, it can be recycled.

HDPE

Used for everyday items such as milk, shampoo, and detergent bottles; drainpipes; gutters; and garden furniture.

Full name High-density polyethylene

Origin HDPE is made from petroleum.

Lifespan It can be repurposed in the garden, such as a carrier for water or to hold feed for birds. It is not biodegradable but is recyclable.

PVC

A rigid, light plastic, PVC is used widely for house and garden functions such as pipes, door and window frames, or greenhouses.

Full name Polyvinyl chloride

Origin PVC is made with chlorine and hydrocarbons.

Lifespan If exposed to high temperatures persistently, PVC will exude harmful chemicals. It requires a specialized recycling process.

PLASTIC WASTE

Unless global changes are made to plastic production and disposal, plastic waste entering the aquatic ecosystem could nearly triple from 10–15 million tons (9–14 million metric tons) in 2016 to 25–41 million tons (23–37 million metric tons) per year by 2040.

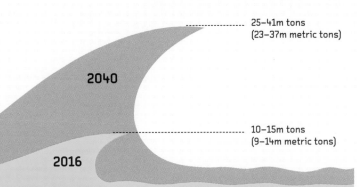

2040

25–41m tons (23–37m metric tons)

2016

10–15m tons (9–14m metric tons)

RECYCLED PLASTIC

In 1950, 1.7 million tons (1.5 million metric tons) of plastic were produced, and all of this went into landfills. By 2020, the amount had increased to a huge 400 million tons (367 million metric tons). Only 9 percent of plastic was recycled; 22 percent of plastic ended up in the natural environment, on land or in water.

1.7m tons (1.5m metric tons) of plastic produced

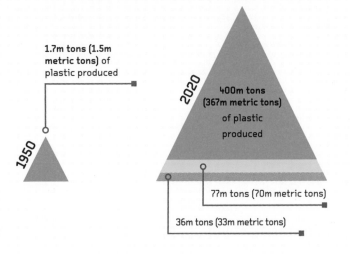

1950

2020

400m tons (367m metric tons) of plastic produced

77m tons (70m metric tons)

36m tons (33m metric tons)

- Landfills/terrestrial or aquatic environments
- Recycled
- Incinerated

LDPE

A flexible, lightweight plastic, this is used in plastic bags, cardboard cup linings, food storage bags, and squeezable bottles.

Full name Low-density polyethylene

Origin LDPE is a thermoplastic made from the monomer ethylene.

Lifespan It can be reused but is difficult to recycle. As a cup lining, it can take 2–20 years to break down.

PP

Used in chip packages and also to make rigid containers such as plant pots, potting trays, and microwaveable meal trays.

Full name Polypropylene, also known as polypropene

Origin PP is a thermoplastic polymer.

Lifespan This plastic can be reused multiple times and is generally able to be recycled, but not if it is black, as this is not recognized by automated sorting machines.

PS

Found in packaging, takeout food boxes, and foam cups.

Full name Polystyrene

Origin Polystyrene is made from the monomer styrene, which is derived from oil, as in the case of most plastics.

Lifespan As polystyrene has been found to be toxic and possibly carcinogenic, it should not be used in the garden. It is not widely recyclable, requiring a specialized process.

OTHER

This category of plastics indicates different resin mixes and also other specialized types of plastic packaging. Many plastics under this umbrella are toxic and should be avoided in the garden or anywhere plants are grown. They cannot usually be recycled.

PLASTIC ALTERNATIVES

UNFORTUNATELY, IT'S STILL ALMOST IMPOSSIBLE TO BE
PLASTIC-FREE IN THE GARDEN AND IN THE HORTICULTURE
INDUSTRY, BUT ALTERNATIVE MATERIALS ARE ARRIVING ON
THE MARKET AND THERE ARE WAYS THAT WE CAN REDUCE
PLASTIC IN THE GARDEN.

PLASTIC-FREE HORTICULTURE?

Everything from bagged compost and gravel to tools, plant pots, and general sundries contains types of plastic. For the Yeo Valley Organic Show Garden, we tried to limit this by using biodegradable rice husk pots—the traditional and widely used black plastic pots are not recyclable, as they contain pigments that make them undetectable to the machinery used to sort plastics. However, they can be reused many times, and a number of nurseries will accept them for reuse. It is also becoming more common to use colored plastic pots so they can be recognized and recycled by sorting machinery.

Other steps toward avoiding waste plastic can be taken, such as getting soils, aggregates, or gravel delivered loose instead of bagged, depending on local conditions and access. Bare-root plants are also becoming more widely used, though these need to be planted out quickly to keep them from drying out and perishing. Tackling plastic use in the horticulture industry will take joined-up thinking; examples include allotment gardeners pooling money to purchase bulk loads of materials and consumers pressurizing suppliers who use excessive or unnecessary plastics in packaging, demanding that they provide viable alternatives.

HOW TO AVOID PLASTIC IN THE GARDEN

• Buy loose materials where possible.
• Buy plants bare root or in pots that are biodegradable.
• Make compost at home.
• Use natural and biodegradable materials such as hazel, willow, bamboo, and natural fiber twine for garden structures.
• Most garden products or tools have a plastic-free alternative, so look at the available range before purchasing.
• Research suppliers and check on their commitments to reducing plastic use and choosing compostable plastics.

These pots are made from rice husks—a waste material in rice production. They provide an alternative to the commonly used black plastic pots, which are not recyclable. Made from plant fiber, bound together using a mixed natural and synthetic compound, they have a smooth finish similar to that of plastic. They are practical, hard-wearing, and reusable and, once composted, they will biodegrade after approximately five years.

BIOPLASTICS

These plastics are produced from renewable organic origins, such as vegetable fats and oils, plants, cornstarch, straw, wood chips, sawdust, and food waste.

Bioplastics can make use of agricultural byproducts, using less fossil fuels than conventional plastics in the manufacturing process and having the capability to biodegrade. Useful formulas are still being refined, but bioplastics are being used more frequently for items such as disposable cutlery, straws, bowls, and packaging.

Some bioplastics are compostable and are even considered to be suitable for putting in a home food compost bin, but they still take time to break down and often require particular conditions, such as heat. Research is still being done into the sort of residual matter they leave behind after they break down, which, as they are a fairly new material, is still relatively unknown.

BIOPLASTIC PRODUCTION

Out of the millions of tons of plastic produced annually, bioplastics make up just 1 percent, but demand for them is growing, and capacity for producing them is set to rise. Global bioplastic production is forecast to reach 7.72 million tons (7.59 million metric tons) in 2026.

● Biodegradable
○ Bio-based/nonbiodegradable
◐ Total amount

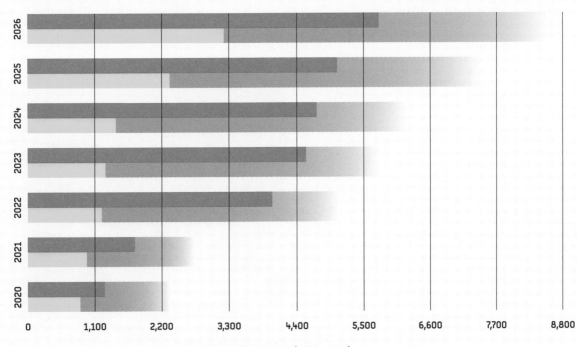

Production (million tons)

01

[01] In this garden, I used hard industrial steel in multiple finishes to offset the soft planting. It is an incredibly versatile, strong, and beautiful material, able to be formed and perforated. [02] Steel has long been used for water features, as it is naturally impermeable. The liquid reflectiveness of the water provides a beautiful counterpoint to the rigid hardness of the steel.
[03] On the roof terrace of the Lemon Tree Trust garden at Chelsea Flower Show in 2018, patterns for zinc planters were laser cut from sheet-thin material and then folded by hand on site. No screws or attachments were needed, and the idea was that the plans could be sent anywhere in the world and produced low cost to create long-lasting, lightweight, and durable planters.

02

METAL

METAL IS A SOLID MATERIAL WITH VARYING LEVELS OF LUSTER THAT CAN BE ALTERED BY POLISHING. IT IS CHARACTERIZED AS EITHER MALLEABLE (CAN BE HAMMERED INTO THIN SHEETS) OR DUCTILE (CAN BE DRAWN OUT INTO THIN WIRES).

METAL IN LANDSCAPING

Versatile and durable, metal can be incorporated into a range of styles and schemes. Rusting and weathering can change its appearance over time, allowing it to settle naturally into its surroundings. It is naturally robust and can be used for large structures such as staircases, pergolas, or laser cut screens, but it is equally good for smaller details like bird feeders or containers. It is generally a heavy, dense material, so its environmental impact is increased by shipping, and manufacture is carbon-intensive.

03

MILD STEEL

In its raw state, iron is soft and therefore not feasible for use as a construction material. The main technique for strengthening iron and transforming it into steel is the incorporation of small levels of carbon. Globally, steel production is one of the most energy-exhaustive and carbon-abundant industries—in 2020, it was responsible for around 7 percent of the world's carbon dioxide emissions. Currently, China produces more steel than the rest of the world put together, making it the global leader by a long way.

Origin Alloy of iron and carbon.

Lifespan Depending on the thickness of the steel and the environmental conditions, mild steel can last for decades.

TYPES OF METAL

SEVERAL METALS ARE SUITABLE FOR USE IN THE GARDEN, BOTH TO FULFILL PRACTICAL FUNCTIONS AND TO PROVIDE VISUAL EFFECTS.

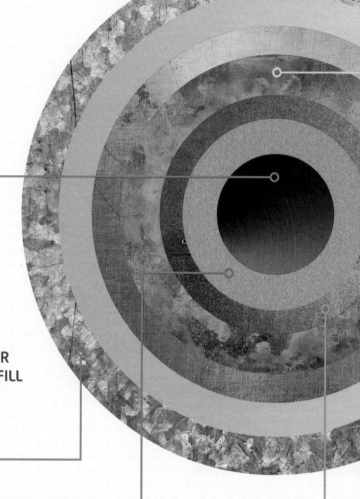

GALVANIZED STEEL

Galvanization is a process where steel is dipped into a vat of molten zinc, creating a protective coating and preventing rust. Zinc can make steel stronger and prolong its life, but high levels of zinc can be harmful to the environment and can pollute water when not properly sanitized during manufacturing.

Origin Steel, zinc

Lifespan Galvanization can deliver 50+ years of protection against rust and corrosion without any maintenance. At the end of its life, galvanized steel can be recycled.

WEATHERING STEEL

The process of manufacturing weathering steel starts with combining iron, copper, chromium, and nickel, with further alloying components such as phosphorus, silicon, and manganese. These facilitate the development of a layer of rust on the surface of the metal that improves resistance to weathering and corrosion.

Origin Weathering steel is an alloy of iron, copper, chromium, and nickel.

Lifespan The lifespan is generally longer the thicker it is, but the protective rust layer means the metal can last for many decades before needing to be replaced.

ZINC

Zinc is extracted by concentrating and heating the ore, then processing it into a usable metal by heating with carbon or using electrolysis.

Origin Zinc is extracted from the earth, with the main sources being zinc sulfide ore and zinc silicate (calamine) ore. The prime mining areas are in China, Australia, and Peru.

Lifespan Zinc reacts with oxygen and carbon dioxide to develop a protective patina, making zinc very durable, and it can last for up to 100 years. At the end of its life, zinc retrieved from modern products can be recycled without deteriorating.

COPPER

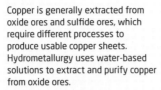

Copper is generally extracted from oxide ores and sulfide ores, which require different processes to produce usable copper sheets. Hydrometallurgy uses water-based solutions to extract and purify copper from oxide ores.

Origin Copper is found in sedimentary and igneous rocks in the form of minerals and ore. El Teniente in Chile is the largest copper mine globally.

Lifespan Copper can last for more than 100 years outside. Waste copper can be resmelted and recycled, which uses less energy than mining for fresh ore. Copper is a finite resource and about a third used globally is recycled.

BRONZE

Bronze is an alloy of copper and tin formed by melting both materials together. Tin is mined from the Earth's crust and is a fairly scarce resource—around half of tin produced today is from Southeast Asia. To extract tin, the mineral cassiterite is heated with carbon in a furnace at very high temperatures.

Origin An alloy of copper and tin.

Lifespan Ancient artifacts are testament to the enduring durability of bronze. While it is recycled, information on energy saved is lacking as bronze is costly, and therefore used less often in construction.

ALUMINUM

Alumina or aluminum oxide is drawn out of bauxite using heat and caustic soda. Bauxite occurs relatively close to the Earth's surface and so is fairly easy to extract. Pure aluminum is produced using electrolytic reduction, which requires huge amounts of electricity, making it an expensive and carbon-heavy process.

Origin Aluminum is one of the most plentiful metals occurring naturally. Around 90 percent of the world's bauxite is located in tropical and subtropical regions, and around 73 percent occurs in five countries: Guinea, Brazil, Jamaica, Australia, and India.

Lifespan Aluminum can last for up to 100 years outside and can be repeatedly recycled without compromising its qualities.

RECYCLING METAL

Almost all metals can be recycled, and this chart shows the percentage of recycled metals consumed in the US in 2007. While bronze is widely recycled, it is less commonly used, so accurate data is not available.

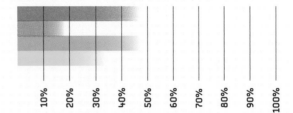

10% 20% 30% 40% 50% 60% 70% 80% 90% 100%

Percentage of metals recycled, US 2017

ENERGY SAVED

Amount of energy saved by recycling compared to extracting the metal from raw. As above, the data is not available for bronze, as it is less commonly used.

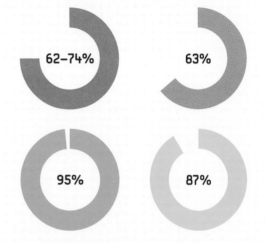

62–74%   63%

95%   87%

COMMON USES

The metals featured here can all be used within our gardens. Steel and aluminum are the most versatile.

Sculptures/ Features	●	●	●	●	●
Planters	●	●	●		
Furniture	●		●		
Edging	●		●		
Cladding	●	●	●	●	●

COMPOST

USUALLY COMPOSED OF RECYCLED ORGANIC MATTER, SUCH AS PLANT AND FOOD WASTE, COMPOST IS USED AS A SOIL IMPROVER AND FERTILIZER. COMPOSTS ARE FULL OF NUTRIENTS TO ENCOURAGE HEALTHY PLANT GROWTH AND ADVANTAGEOUS ORGANISMS, SUCH AS EARTHWORMS AND FUNGAL MYCELIUM.

01

Valued at $5,592.3 million in 2020, and forecast to reach $7,516.5 million by the end of 2027, the global compost market is huge and continues to grow. Although compost is used to cultivate and sustain plant life, the production of it is not always without controversy or environmental impact.

THE ROLE OF PEAT

Peat is used as a component of many commercially sold composts as a soil improver and for potting up seedlings. It has long been a popular material for compost, as it can provide ideal conditions for establishing young plants, being free-draining but also remaining moist.

However, it has been apparent for a long time that the extraction of peat from the land is damaging to the environment. Consisting of partly decayed vegetation and other organic material, peat is formed over many generations. For peat to develop, the vegetation must be buried in waterlogged soils with little or no access to oxygen, which stops the organic material from decomposing completely. Peat is found specifically in natural peatlands, including moors, bogs, and fens. These peatlands occur globally; the largest area of peatland in the world is the tropical Cuvette Centrale peatland in the central Congo basin, covering an area of 56,178 sq miles (145,500 sq km), more than the area of England.

Peatlands are the most effective carbon sinks (an area that absorbs more carbon than is released) in the world; a natural balance is sustained because peatland plants absorb the carbon dioxide naturally exuding from the peat. When peat is extracted for commercial use, not only are large amounts of carbon dioxide released, the local flora and fauna are destroyed. In the UK, peat is to be banned from use in home gardening.

03

02

[01] At this peat extraction site, the landscape is bare and devoid of life. The use of peat is damaging to the environment and therefore a problematic material in the garden. [02] In order to collect peat, the upper surface of the peatland is removed, destroying unique and threatened flora and fauna while also liberating huge amounts of carbon dioxide into the atmosphere. [03] Viru Bog at Lahemaa National Park, Estonia, is protected and thriving. To preserve the vegetation and peat-rich soil, visitors must stay on the boardwalks.

235

PEAT-FREE ALTERNATIVES

ALTERNATIVES TO PEAT COMPOST ARE AVAILABLE AND ENCOMPASS BLENDS OF DECAYED ORGANIC MATTER SUCH AS BARK, COCONUT FIBER, AND WOOD CHIPS. THEY CAN BE COMBINED WITH INORGANIC MATERIAL INCLUDING GRIT, SHARP SAND, ROCK WOOL, AND PERLITE.

Most of the alternatives to peat are easily sourced, and some are even available without any cost. Making use of them in the garden keeps some from going to landfills, too.

SHEEP'S WOOL WASTE

Wool improves water retention and provides a slow release of nitrogen into the soil as well as acting as a weed-suppressant and regulating temperature. It is considered a sustainable, eco-friendly alternative to using peat. Available from garden centers and online, it can be incorporated in the soil or used as a mulch on the surface.

BRACKEN

Fresh green bracken fronds can be put on a compost heap, where they will enhance the nutrients in the compost as they rot down. Avoid the roots, as they can germinate and create new plants. In the fall, dead bracken can be broken down to make mulch in the same way as leaf mold (see opposite).

WOOD FIBER

Used as a mulch, woody matter such as sawdust or composted bark can improve the soil's ability to retain moisture. It is most sustainable and cheapest when acquired as a locally sourced untreated wood byproduct.

PINE NEEDLES

Abundant and easily obtained, these are best used as a mulch on top of the soil, where they can bond together as a permeable mat that is not easily blown away. While they can change the texture of the soil, they do not retain water or hugely affect nutrient levels.

COMPOSTED MANURE

Manure is one of the most effective alternatives to peat, as it improves the important microbes in the soil, aids plant growth, and increases moisture

01

02

03

04

[1] Sheep's wool waste
[2] Bracken
[3] Wood fiber
[4] Pine needles

retention. Fresh manure is very acidic and contains high levels of nitrogen, which can have a negative impact on plants, so it should be composted down before application. Bagged, composted manure is widely available.

LEAF MOLD

As leaf mold is created when dead leaves are left to rot down, it is an inexpensive, renewable, and locally available resource. All that is required is for leaves to be piled up and turned over periodically in order to speed up the decomposition process. When added to the soil, leaf mold can aid moisture retention and supply nutrients.

BIOCHAR

This soil improver is produced through pyrolysis (heating to very high temperatures without oxygen). Like charcoal, it can be made from organic substances, generally wood. When organic material breaks down, the inherent carbon is released into the atmosphere. Biochar decomposes very slowly, over hundreds of years, so organic material converted into biochar essentially sequesters the inherent carbon, preventing it from being released. It is extremely moisture-retentive and good at retaining nutrients, so it is an ideal soil improver. Available online, it can be incorporated into compost mixes or used on directly on the soil as a mulch.

COIR (COCONUT FIBER)

Composed of the fibers found between the flesh layer and the shell of coconuts, coir is used for many products such as doormats and brushes, but leftover short fibers act as a peat alternative. As it can hold up to 10 times its weight in water, it is extremely efficient at retaining moisture. The harvesting and shipping means it is not the ideal peat replacement, but as it is a byproduct of coconuts already grown for eating, it is a more sustainable option than peat.

RICE HULLS

Hulls are the outer layer of rice grains removed before the rice is packaged for eating. They are usually thrown away but can be used as a valuable soil improver, as they help incorporate air in the soil and retain water. They add nutrients to the soil as they rot down, improving conditions for a full growing season. Available online, they can also be found in some garden supply stores.

05

[5] Composted manure
[6] Leaf mold
[7] Biochar
[8] Coir
[9] Rice hulls

06

07

08

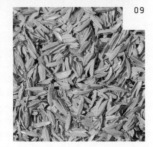

09

INNOVATIVE MATERIALS

LOOKING INTO THE FUTURE, THERE ARE MANY NEW AND EXCITING MATERIALS BEING ENGINEERED FOR USE IN LANDSCAPES, BUILDINGS, AND GARDENS. SOME KEEP WASTE FROM BEING SENT TO LANDFILLS AND BREATHE NEW LIFE INTO OTHERWISE DISCARDED MATTER, WHILE OTHERS ENGINEER NATURE FOR HUMAN BENEFIT.

INNOVATIVE PAVING

Manufacturers are finding ways of combining environmental solutions and functional surfaces. For example, AquiPor Technologies has created a permeable concrete that filters out harmful pollutants as storm water flows through it, combating urban flooding from increased rainfall; Pavegen has developed paving that generates electricity using kinetic energy from footsteps as it is walked on.

RECYCLED MATERIALS

Incorporating waste and recycled materials into new sustainable products serves a dual purpose. In the Netherlands, Stone Cycling collects and processes debris from construction and demolition, turning waste material into new bricks. Recycled plastics are also being used to create products such as decking, sheet materials, and garden furniture.

ENGINEERED TIMBER PRODUCTS

Modern processes have been formulated to improve the lifespan and properties of natural wood, ranging from thermally treating to pickling. Accoya wood is mature softwood species such as pine treated with acetic acid to give it the properties of a hardwood, creating a rot-resistant material that can be recycled just like natural timber. Tricoya uses the same process to treat MDF. Transparent wood composites are new wood materials which have up to 90 percent transparency and are much more biodegradable than glass and plastic.

MANURE

Animal manure is a familiar garden staple, found globally in abundance. Merdacotta has given it a new lease of life, using cow dung, clay, straw, and farm waste to produce flower pots and tiles that have a terracottalike finish but are lighter and more resistant to fluctuating climates. The Mestic project discovered a process to extract cellulose from dung and use it to make biomaterial products such as paper, textiles, and bioplastics.

FUNGAL MATERIAL

Mycelium, the fast-growing, underground network of fungi, is being used in innovative design. New York design practice The Living worked on the Hy-Fi project, a temporary mycelium brick tower at the Museum of Modern Art. Formed in molds in less than a week, the bricks were composted once the structure was dismantled. Italian design firm Carlo Ratti Associati created the Circular Garden, a series of arches formed by injecting fungal spores into organic material, while Officina Corpuscoli, a multidisciplinary design studio, supports multiple projects dedicated to evolving mycelium-based technology.

[01] The organic brick structure known as "Hy-Fi" was designed by David Benjamin of New York architects The Living. It is built from organic, biodegradable bricks consisting of cultures of fungus and farm waste grown to fit a brick-shaped mold.

[02] Stone Cycling aim to prove that it's possible to build high-quality, aesthetic materials from waste. Their WasteBasedBricks are made from waste materials and are extensively tested to ensure success. [03] In Sarah Eberle's 2022 Chelsea Garden, a waterfall inspired by natural rock strata cascaded into a pool. It was constructed of Tricoya, made to look like stone. More durable than standard timber materials, Tricoya can be used for wider applications, including those that require a higher degree of moisture resistance, such as this water feature.

GLOSSARY

AIR POLLUTION
Harmful chemicals or particles in the air, often derived from vehicular traffic or industry.

BIODEGRADABLE
Describes substances that decay naturally without causing harm to the environment.

BIODIVERSITY
Also known as biological diversity or species richness, the variety of life found in a particular place or on Earth generally. A common measure of this is the count of species in a specified area.

BIODIVERSITY CRISIS
The rapid loss of species and degradation of ecosystems caused by human actions that have a negative impact upon them.

BIOMATERIAL
A substance that is derived from or produced by biological organisms, such as plants and animals, and can be used as a material for making things or as fuel.

BIOME
A large area of land and the particular combination of climate, plants, and animals that are found in it.

BIOSECURITY
Measures to prevent the introduction and/or spread of harmful organisms to animals and plants.

CARBON CAPTURE
A way of collecting the carbon dioxide (CO_2) emissions produced from industrial processes or the burning of fossil fuels so that it is not released into the air.

CARBON DIOXIDE EQUIVALENT (CO_2E)
The number of metric tons of CO_2 emissions with the same global warming potential as 1 metric ton of another greenhouse gas.

CARBON FOOTPRINT
A measure of the total greenhouse gas emissions caused directly and indirectly by a person, organization, event, or product.

CARBON NEUTRAL
Causing no net release of carbon dioxide into the atmosphere, especially as a result of carbon offsetting.

CARBON OFFSET
A reduction in emissions of carbon dioxide or other greenhouse gases or an increase in carbon storage used to compensate for emissions that occur elsewhere. Offsets are measured in metric tons of carbon dioxide equivalent (CO_2e). One metric ton of carbon offset represents the reduction of 1 metric ton of carbon dioxide or its equivalent in other greenhouse gases.

CARBON SEQUESTRATION
The capture and secure storage of carbon that would otherwise be emitted to the atmosphere. It is also referred to as "carbon draw-down."

CIRCULAR PLASTIC
The process of keeping existing plastic in use for as long as possible by recovering and regenerating it to make new products, thus extracting the maximum value from it.

CLIMATE CRISIS
The highly dangerous, irreversible changes to the global climate resulting from global warming, causing problems such as environmental degradation, natural disasters, weather extremes, food and water insecurity, and economic disruption.

CLIMATE POSITIVE
A commitment to go beyond net zero (see below) by investing in nature-based solutions that will make a net beneficial impact on the climate.

CLIMATE RESILIENCE
The ability to prepare for and respond to hazardous events, disturbances, or trends that are related to climate. Improving climate resilience requires assessing how climate change will engender new or alter current climate-related risks and taking steps to lessen these risks through adaptation and mitigation.

CULTIVATED PLANT DIVERSITY
A mixture of native and cultivated plants grown in gardens or landscapes.

ECOLOGICAL GARDENING
Gardening with a natural balance for wildlife and human well-being, including herbicide- and pesticide-free management.

FOREST GARDEN
A designed agronomic system using trees, shrubs, and perennial plants in a way that echoes the structure of a natural forest.

FOSSIL FUELS

Fuels such as coal and natural gas formed from organic matter laid down millions of years ago that fossilized, creating an underground carbon store. When these fuels are burned, CO_2 is released.

GRAY WATER

Previously used domestic water that contains no fecal matter and can be stored and reused, for example, for watering.

GREENHOUSE EFFECT

An increase in the amount of carbon dioxide and other gases in the atmosphere (mixture of gases around the Earth) that causes a warming of the surface of the Earth.

GREENHOUSE GAS (GHG) EMISSIONS

Gases discharged into the Earth's atmosphere as a result of human activity that are accelerating global warming, especially carbon dioxide resulting from the burning of fossil fuels.

HEAT SINK

A substance or an object that absorbs heat.

NATURE-BASED SOLUTIONS

Actions to protect, sustainably manage, and restore natural or modified ecosystems to benefit both human well-being and biodiversity.

NET EMISSIONS REDUCTION

Reducing annual greenhouse gas emissions with projects that prevent or reduce emissions.

NET POSITIVE

Putting back more into society, the environment, and the global economy than is taken out.

NET ZERO

Of a country, city, and so on, removing as many emissions of gases that cause global warming as it produces.

PASSIVE IRRIGATION SYSTEM

A system by which the runoff from rain is directed to landscapes, either at the surface (where the water filters down through the soil) or through subsurface systems that recharge soil moisture at a depth where plant roots can access it.

PEAT

An accumulation of partially decayed organic matter, peat is unique to natural areas called peatlands, bogs, mires, moors, or muskegs.

PLANETARY BOUNDARIES

Introduced in 2009, the Planetary Boundaries concept aimed to define the environmental limits within which humanity can safely operate and has influenced the development of global sustainability policy.

RAINWATER HARVESTING

In a rainwater harvesting system, water is collected and stored in a tank and then pumped to direct the water where it is needed in the home.

RENEWABLE ENERGY

Energy produced by natural and self-replenishing resources, such as sunlight, wind, rain, waves, tides, geothermal heat, and bioenergy derived by burning organic material.

REWILDING

The process of protecting an environment and returning it to its original state by letting natural processes shape the landscape and bringing back wild animals that used to live there.

SUBSTRATE

The surface on which a plant lives; the soil is the substrate of most plants.

SUSTAINABILITY

The integration of environmental health, social equity, and economic vitality to create thriving, diverse, and resilient communities for the present and future.

SWALE

A low-lying or depressed and often wet and vegetated stretch of land. Artificial swales are often infiltration channels designed to manage water runoff, filter pollutants, and increase rainwater infiltration.

UN COP SUMMIT

The United Nations Climate Change Conference of the Parties (COP) attended by representatives from different countries.

WATER-NEUTRAL

Where total water use is equal to or less than total natural water supply. This involves using less water and capturing, reusing, and recycling water.

ZERO WASTE

At least 99 percent of generated waste is diverted away from landfills, which means that all waste produced is reused, recycled, composted, or sent to energy recovery.

FURTHER READING

ENDNOTES

Chapter 1

10 Richmond Park is a site of both national and international importance for wildlife conservation: The Royal Parks, 2019.
frp.org.uk/wp-content/uploads/2019/01/RICHMOND-PARK-DESIGNATIONS-NNR-SSSI-SAC-and-Listed-Buildings.pdf

11 A scene typical of Richmond Park, which contains an estimated 1,300 veteran oak trees: Friends of Richmond Park, 2018.
frp.org.uk/ancient-oaks-in-the-park

11 There are an estimated 3 billion yellow meadow ants residing in Richmond Park: The Royal Parks.
royalparks.org.uk/media-centre/press-releases/eye-popping-stats-show-billions-of-ants-re-designing-one-of-europes-most-important-parks

Chapter 2

26 In February 2022, the Royal Society in London published a report that looked at the first flowering times of plants, using more than 400,000 studies and starting as far back as 1753: "Plants in the UK Flower a Month Earlier Under Recent Warming," Ulf Büntgen, Alma Piermattei, Paul J. Krusic, Jan Esper, Tim Sparks, and Alan Crivellaro, 2022.
royalsocietypublishing.org/doi/10.1098/rspb.2021.2456

26 Solastalgia is a word coined by Glenn Albrecht: "'Solastalgia': a new concept in health and identity," Glenn Albrecht, 2016.
bridges.monash.edu/articles/journal_contribution/_Solastalgia_a_new_concept_in_health_and_identity/4311905

28 If every UK gardener planted a medium-sized tree, these trees would store carbon the equivalent of driving 11.4 million times around the planet: RHS, 2021.
rhs.org.uk/about-the-rhs/sustainability/sustainability-strategy-document

29 The American Psychology Association (APA) describes eco-anxiety: "Mental Health and our Changing Climate: Impacts, Implications, And Guidance," Susan Clayton Whitmore-Williams, Christie Manning, Kirra Krygsman, Meighen Speiser, 2017.
apa.org/news/press/releases/2017/03/mental-health-climate.pdf

30 There are more than 30 million people involved in gardening in the UK alone: RHS.
rhs.org.uk/get-involved/wild-about-gardens

31 The total area of gardens in the UK is estimated at approximately 1,670 square miles (433,000 hectares): Wildlife Gardening Forum.
wlgf.org/The%20garden%20Resource.pdf

38 A report that was issued in 2021 by the Intergovernmental Panel on Climate Change (IPCC) attested to the fact that we are in a state of climate catastrophe: "Climate Change 2021: The Physical Science Basis," IPCC, 2021.
ipcc.ch/report/ar6/wg1/

38 Global climate change map: "Understanding Climate Change from a Global Analysis of City Analogues," Jean-Francois Bastin, Emily Clark, Thomas Elliott, Simon Hart et al., 2019.
doi.org/10.1371/journal.pone.0217592

41 It is estimated that if we continue to emit these gases at the present rate, there could be a temperature rise of 4.5–9°F (2.5–5°C) by the end of the century. With a turn toward sustainable energy, this could drop to a rise of 0.4–3.1°F (0.25–1.75°C): "Climate Change 2021: The Physical Science Basis," IPCC, 2021.
ipcc.ch/report/ar6/wg1/

41 In 2019, the Oxford Dictionary word of the year was "climate emergency": Oxford University Press, 2022.
languages.oup.com/word-of-the-year/2019/

42 An interactive map is available that details the future climates of 530 cities across the world and links them to those that have their anticipated 2050 climate in the present day: OpenStreetMap, Bastin et al., 2019.
hooge104.shinyapps.io/future_cities_app

42 The IPCC's third report installment states that without immediate and deep reductions of emissions across all sectors, limiting global warming to 2.7°F (1.5°C) is beyond reach: "Climate Change 2022: Impacts, Adaptation and Vulnerability," IPCC, 2022.
www.ipcc.ch/report/sixth-assessment-report-working-group-ii

42 "The decisions we make now can secure a liveable future," said IPCC Chair Hoesung Lee: IPCC, 2022.
ipcc.ch/2022/04/04/ipcc-ar6-wgiii-pressrelease

43 At the climate change conference COP21 in Paris in 2015, an international treaty was signed with the goal of limiting global warming to below 3.6°F (2°C): United Nations Climate Change.
unfccc.int/process-and-meetings/the-paris-agreement/the-paris-agreement#

43 COP26 in Glasgow in 2021 failed to reassert the goals for 2030: UN News, 2021.
news.un.org/en/story/2021/11/1105792

45 "Healthy ecosystems are more resilient to climate change and provide life-critical services," said IPCC Working Group II co-chair professor Hans-Otto Pörtner: IPCC, 2022.
ipcc.ch/2022/02/28/pr-wgii-ar6/

48 Psychoanalyst Erich Fromm introduced the word "biophilia" in his book *The Anatomy of*

242

Human Destructiveness. He described it as the "passionate love of life and of all that is alive … whether in a person, a plant, an idea, or a social group." Fromm, Erich, *The Anatomy of Human Destructiveness* (Holt, Rinehart and Winston, 1973)

51 Every 2¼lb (1kg) of site-made compost typically saves 3½oz (100g of carbon dioxide emissions: RHS, 2021.
rhs.org.uk/about-the-rhs/sustainability/sustainability-strategy-document

53 Green roof systems can be incorporated into any structures to increase biodiversity and sequester carbon: "Carbon Sequestration Potential of Extensive Green Roofs," Kristin L. Getter, D. Bradley Rowe, G. Philip Robertson, Bert M. Cregg, and Jeffrey A. Andresen, 2009.
pubs.acs.org/doi/abs/10.1021/es901539x

53 Cut flowers and foliage can save up to 17½lb (7.9kg) carbon per bunch compared to buying imported or commercially produced bunches: RHS, 2021.
rhs.org.uk/about-the-rhs/sustainability/sustainability-strategy-document

54 Sir Robert Watson, chair of the Intergovernmental Science-Policy Platform on Biodiversity and Ecosystem Services, states "We are eroding the very foundations of our economies, livelihoods, food security, health, and quality of life worldwide": United Nations, 2019.
un.org/sustainabledevelopment/blog/2019/05/nature-decline-unprecedented-report/

55 Professor Dave Goulson states: "Insects make up about two-thirds of all life on Earth [but] there has been some kind of horrific decline": *The Guardian*, 2018.
theguardian.com/environment/2018/jun/17/where-have-insects-gone-climate-change-population-decline

59 An example of a bacterial disease that has damaging effects on a wide range of plants is *Xylella fastidiosa*: Megan Bickle, 2019.
planthealthportal.defra.gov.uk/assets/uploads/EvidenceStatement-XylellaFastidiosa.pdf

Chapter 3
64 The urban heat island effect can cause temperatures in cities to rise by 9°F (5°C): World Meteorological Organization, 2020.
community.wmo.int/activity-areas/urban/urban-heat-island

66 In the UK, the RHS offers a soil analysis service: RHS, 2022.
rhs.org.uk/membership/rhs-gardening-advice/soil-analysis-service

68 Identifying soil types: RHS, 2022.
rhs.org.uk/soil-composts-mulches/soil-types

70 Testing the acidity/alkalinity of your soil: RHS, 2022.
rhs.org.uk/soil-composts-mulches/ph-and-testing-soil

79 By 2050, 5 billion people could be affected by water shortages: "The United Nations World Water Development Report 2018: Nature-Based Solutions For Water," UNESCO World Water Assessment Programme, 2018.
unesdoc.unesco.org/ark:/48223/pf0000261424

79 More than 2 billion of the world's population do not have safe drinking water available in their homes: World Health Organization, 2019.
who.int/news/item/18-06-2019-1-in-3-people-globally-do-not-have-access-to-safe-drinking-water-unicef-who

79 SuDS imitate a flow of water similar to that of a nondeveloped site, expelling water into the surrounding environment in a regulated way: Local Government Association, 2022.
local.gov.uk/topics/severe-weather/flooding/sustainable-drainage-systems

79 In the UK in 2020, there were more than 400,000 discharges of untreated sewage into rivers and almost 5,500 discharges into UK coastal bathing waters: Surfers Against Sewage, 2022.
sas.org.uk/water-quality

81 Types of sun and shade: RHS, 2022.
rhs.org.uk/garden-design/shade-gardening

82 Understanding wind and temperature: National Geographic, 2022.
education.nationalgeographic.org/resource/wind

84 Windbreaks and shelterbelts: RHS, 2022.
rhs.org.uk/plants/types/hedges/windbreaks-shelterbelts

89 "Green walls" have the capacity to reduce pollution by 30 percent: "The Effectiveness of Green Infrastructure for Improvement of Air Quality in Urban Street Canyons," Pugh, T. A. M., A. R. MacKenzie, J. D. Whyatt, and C. N. Hewitt, 2012.
birmingham.ac.uk/news/2012/researching-the-air-pollution-filtering-effects-of-green-walls-1

Chapter 4
96 Heat islands in cities: United States Environmental Protection Programme, 2022.
epa.gov/heatislands/learn-about-heat-islands

108 Installing a green roof: RHS, 2022.
rhs.org.uk/garden-features/green-roofs

114 Planting a food forest, or forest garden: Centre for Alternative Technology (CAT), 2022.
cat.org.uk/info-resources/free-information-service/growing-and-eating/forest-garden/

118 British organic gardener Charles Dowding is a pioneer of the no-dig approach: Charles Dowding, 2022.
charlesdowding.co.uk

122 The microorganisms that transform waste material into compost work most effectively at consistent levels of temperature and moisture: RHS, 2022.
rhs.org.uk/soil-composts-mulches/composting

125 Homemade garden compost is usually ready to use in six months to two years: RHS, 2022.
rhs.org.uk/soil-composts-mulches/composting

126 The benefits of mulching: RHS, 2022.
rhs.org.uk/soil-composts-mulches/mulch

132 The value of sustainable drainage systems (SuDS): HebdenBridge.org, 2019.
hebdenbridge.org/slow-the-flow-nfm-and-suds-opportunity-mapping-in-mytholmroyd-west-yorkshire/

133 An online resource explains how water usage in gardens can be reduced: RHS and Cranfield University.
mains2rains.uk/

134 Storm water management: Water Network Research, 2020.
thewaternetwork.com/article-FfV/changing-the-nature-of-storm-watermanagement-l1A2YatvIwd4FJZAE4G3Fw

139 Creating a windbreak in your garden with wind-resilient species: RHS, 2022.
rhs.org.uk/plants/types/hedges/windbreaks-shelterbelts

139 Plants can assist in capturing particulate pollution: RHS, 2022.
rhs.org.uk/science/articles/super-cotoneaster

146 Hugelkultur mounds: Permaculture, 2022.
permaculture.co.uk/articles/the-many-benefits-of-hugelkultur/

148 Wabi-sabi is a Japanese ideology embracing that which is imperfect and ephemeral to be found in the natural world: Koren, Leonard, *Wabi-Sabi for Artists, Designers, Poets and Philosophers*, (Stone Bridge Press, 1994)

150 The growth of saprophytic fungi: RHS, 2022.
rhs.org.uk/biodiversity/saprophytic-fungi

151 Ash dieback has caused widespread damage to ash trees across Europe for 20 years: Woodland Trust, 2022.
woodlandtrust.org.uk/trees-woods-and-wildlife/tree-pests-and-diseases/key-tree-pests-and-diseases/ash-dieback/

152 Growing shiitake on hardwood logs: Urban Farm-It, 2022.
urban-farm-it.com/how-to-grow-mushrooms/

155 Sounds in nature may have a positive impact on our mental health: BBC, 2022.
bbc.co.uk/news/uk-england-devon-60840759

Chapter 6

211 Lifecycle flow chart: Adapted from Figure 5.2, 'LETI Embodied Carbon Primer: Supplementary guidance to the Climate Emergency Design Guide', Alex Johnstone et al, 2020.
leti.uk/_files/
ugd/252d09_8ceffcbcafdb43cf8a19ab9af5073b92.pdf

215 Carbon storing capacity chart: Visual Capitalist, 2022.
visualcapitalist.com/sp/visualizing-carbon-storage-in-earths-ecosystems

216 Igneous rocks form when magma or lava from beneath the Earth's crust cools and then solidifies: National Geographic, 2022.
education.nationalgeographic.org/resource/igneous-rocks

220 Recycled gravel infographic adapted from: "Global CO_2 Emissions from Cement Production," Andrew, R. M., Earth Syst. Sci. Data, 10, 195–217, fig.2, doi.org/10.5194/essd-10-195-2018, 2018, CC BY 4.0.

222 China is estimated to have produced half of the world's cement in 2021: "Leading Cement Producing Countries Worldwide 2021," M. Garside, 2022.
statista.com/statistics/267364/world-cement-production-by-country/#statisticContainer

222 It is thought that concrete uses nearly 10 percent of global industrial water consumption and accounts for 4–8 percent of CO_2 emissions globally: *The Guardian*, 2019.
theguardian.com/cities/2019/feb/25/concrete-the-most-destructive-material-on-earth

222 Production of clinker is thought to account for 50 percent of concrete's CO_2 emissions: "Making Concrete Change: Innovation in Low-carbon Cement and Concrete," Johanna Lehne and Felix Preston, 2018.
chathamhouse.org/sites/default/files/publications/2018-06-13-making-concrete-change-cement-lehne-preston-final.pdf

223 Cement production infographic: Heidrich, Craig & Hinczak, Ihor & Ryan, Bridget. (2022). SCM's potential to lower Australia's greenhouse gas emissions profile.

223 Growing emissions chart: Earth System Science Data adapted from: "Global CO_2 emissions from cement production," Andrew, R. M., Earth Syst. Sci. Data, 10, 195–217, fig.2, doi.org/10.5194/essd-10-195-2018, 2018, CC BY 4.0

224 Green concrete uses less energy to produce and can be more durable than conventional concrete: "Toward Green Concrete for Better Sustainable Environment," BambangSuhendro, 2014.
sciencedirect.com/science/article/pii/S1877705814032494

224 Rammed earth has a carbon footprint around 40 times lower than concrete: Friends & Co., 2020.
friendsandco.co.uk/is-rammed-earth-the-building-material-of-the-future

225 Natural resources infographic: DB Group, 2022.
dbgholdings.com/cemfree/

227 Plastic waste infographic: UN Environment Programme, 2022.
unep.org/interactives/beat-plastic-pollution

227 Recycled plastic infographic: "Global plastic production 1950–2020," Ian Tiseo, 2022.
statista.com/statistics/282732/global-production-of-plastics-since-1950/

229 Bioplastic production chart: European Bioplastics, nova-Institute, 2021.

233 Recycling metal chart: USGS, 2022, with data courtesy of the British Metals Recycling Association.
usgs.gov/centers/national-minerals-information-center/recycling-statistics-and-information

233 Energy saved infographic: University of Cambridge, 2022.
doitpoms.ac.uk/tlplib/recycling-metals/what.php

234 Valued at US $5,592.3 million in 2020, the global compost market is huge and continues to grow: Digital Journal, 2022.
digitaljournal.com/pr/compost-market-size-in-2022

234 The largest area of peatland in the world is the tropical Cuvette Centrale peatland in the central Congo basin: *The Guardian*, 2017.
theguardian.com/environment/2017/jan/11/worlds-largest-

peatland-vast-carbon-storage-capacity-found-congo

238 Peat-free alternatives: RHS, 2022.
rhs.org.uk/science/gardening-in-a-changing-world/
peat-use-in-gardens/peat-alternatives

238 AquiPor Technologies has created a
permeable concrete:
aquipor.com

238 Pavegen has developed paving that generates
electricity using kinetic energy from footsteps:
pavegen.com

238 Stone Cycling turns waste material into
new bricks:
stonecycling.com/wastebasedbricks

238 Accoya wood is mature softwood species treated
with acetic acid to give it the properties of a hardwood:
accoya.com.

238 Tricoya uses the same process to treat MDF:
tricoya.com

238 Merdacotta uses cow dung, clay, straw, and farm
waste to produce flower pots and tiles:
theshitmuseum.org/prodotti/i-prodotti-da-tavola/

238 The Mestic project discovered a process to extract
cellulose from dung and use it to make biomaterial
products such as paper, textiles, and bioplastics:
inspidere.com

238 New York design practice The Living worked on
the Hy-Fi project, a temporary mycelium brick tower
at the Museum of Modern Art: The Living, 2014.
thelivingnewyork.com

238 Italian design firm Carlo Ratti Associati created
the Circular Garden, a series of arches formed by
injecting fungal spores into organic material: Carlo
Ratti Associati, 2019.
carloratti.com/project/the-circular-garden

238 Officina Corpuscoli, a multidisciplinary design
studio, supports multiple projects dedicated to
evolving mycelium-based technology:
corpuscoli.com

BIBLIOGRAPHY

Books
Boswall, Marian *Sustainable Garden: Projects,
Insights and Advice for the Eco-conscious Gardener*
(Frances Lincoln, 2022)

Chatto, Beth *Beth Chatto's Gravel Garden:
Drought-Resistant Planting Through the Year*
(Francis Lincoln, 2000)

Chatto, Beth *Beth Chatto's Green Tapestry
Revisited: A Guide to a Sustainably Planted Garden*
(Berry & Co., 2021)

Chatto, Beth *Beth Chatto's Shade Garden: Shade-
Loving Plants for Year-Round Interest* (Pimpernel
Press, 2017)

Chatto, Beth *Drought-Resistant Planting:
Lessons from Beth Chatto's Gravel Garden*
(Francis Lincoln, 2016)

Chatto, Beth *The Damp Garden* (W&N, 2018)

Chatto, Beth *The Dry Garden* (W&N, 2018)

Crawford, Martin *Creating a Forest Garden: Working
with Nature to Grow Edible Crops* (Green Books, 2010)

Crawford, Martin *How to Grow Perennial Vegetables:
Low-Maintenance, Low-Impact Vegetable Gardening*
(Green Books, 2012)

Crawford, Martin *Shrubs for Gardens, Agroforestry
and Permaculture* (Permanent Publications, 2020)

Crawford, Martin *Trees for Gardens, Orchards and
Permaculture* (Permanent Publications, 2015)

Crawford, Martin and Aitken, Caroline *Food from
Your Forest Garden: How to Harvest, Cook and
Preserve Your Forest Garden Produce*
(Green Books, 2013)

Dunnett, Nigel *Naturalistic Planting Design: the
Essential Guide* (Filbert Press, 2019)

Dunnett, Nigel *Planting Green Roofs and Living
Walls* (Timber Press, 2008)

Dunnett, Nigel and Clayton, Andy *Rain Gardens*
(Timber Press, 2007)

Dunnett, Nigel, Gedge, Dusty, and Little, John
Small Green Roofs: Low-Tech Options for Homeowners
(Timber Press, 2011)

Dunnett, Nigel and Hitchmough, James (editors)
*The Dynamic Landscape: Design, Ecology and
Management of Naturalistic Urban Planting* (Taylor
& Francis, 2004)

Filippi, Olivier *Bringing the Mediterranean Into Your
Garden: How to Capture the Natural Beauty of the
Mediterranean Garrigue* (Filbert Press, 2019)

Filippi, Olivier *Planting Design for Dry Gardens:
Beautiful, Resilient Groundcovers for Terraces, Paved
Areas, Gravel and Other Alternatives to the Lawn*
(Filbert Press, 2016)

Filippi, Olivier *The Dry Gardening Handbook:
Plants and Practices for a Changing Climate*
Filbert Press, 2019

Franklin, Kate and Till, Caroline *Radical Matter:
Rethinking Materials for a Sustainable Future*
(Thames and Hudson, 2019)

Fromm, Erich *The Anatomy of Human Destructiveness*
(Pimlico 1997)

Golden, James *The View from Federal Twist: A New
Way of Thinking About Gardens, Nature and
Ourselves* (Filbert Press, 2021)

Hitchmough, James *Sowing Beauty* (Timber Press, 2017)

Hitchmough, James and Cameron, Ross
*Environmental Horticulture: Science and Management
of Green Landscapes* (CABI, 2016)

Kingsbury, Noel *Wild, The Naturalistic Garden*
(Phaidon Press, 2022)

Koren, Leonard *Wabi-Sabi: For Artists, Designers,
Poets and Philosophers* (Stone Bridge Press, 2003)

Miles, Ellen (editor) *Nature is a Human Right: Why
We're Fighting for Green in a Grey World* (DK, 2022)

Nex, Sally *RHS How to Garden the Low-carbon Way: The Steps You Can Take to Help Combat Climate Change* (DK, 2021)

Oudolf, Piet and Kingsbury, Noel *Planting: A New Perspective* (Timber Press, 2013)

Rainer, Thomas and West, Claudia *Planting in a Post-Wild World* (Timber Press, 2015)

Rees-Warren, Matt *The Ecological Gardener: How to Create Beauty and Biodiversity from the Soil Up* (Chelsea Green Publishing Co., 2021)

Tree, Isabella *Wilding: The Return of Nature to a British Farm* (Picador, 2019)

Wallington, Jack *Wild About Weeds: Garden Design with Rebel Plants* (Laurence King Publishing, 2019)

Papers

"Climate Change 2021 The Physical Science Basis," 2021.
ipcc.ch/report/ar6/wg1/downloads/report/IPCC_AR6_WGI_Full_Report.pdf

"Efficient Removal of Ultrafine Particles from Diesel Exhaust by Selected Tree Species: Implications for Roadside Planting for Improving the Quality of Urban Air," Huixia Wang, Barbara A. Maher, Imad A. M. Ahmed, and Brian Davison, 2019.
pubs.acs.org/doi/pdf/10.1021/acs.est.8b06629

"Evaluating the Effectiveness of Urban Hedges as Air Pollution Barriers: Importance of Sampling Method, Species Characteristics and Site Location," Tijana Blanuša, Zeenat Jabeen Qadir, Amanpreet Kaur, James Hadley, and Mark B. Gush, 2020.
mdpi.com/2076-3298/7/10/81

"Great Dixter Biodiversity Audit 2017–2019," prepared by Andy Phillips for the Great Dixter Charitable Trust, 2020.
greatdixter.co.uk/great-dixter-biodiversity-audit

"Impact of Sand Extraction from the Bottom of the Southern Baltic Sea on the Relief and Sediments of the Seabed," Szymon Uscinowicz, Wojciech Jeglinski, Grazyna Miotk-Szpiganowicz, Jarosław Nowak, Urszula Paczek, Piotr Przezdziecki, Kazimierz Szefler, Grzegorz Poreba, 2014.
sciencedirect.com/science/article/pii/S0078323414500504

"Mental Health and Our Changing Climate," Susan Clayton Whitmore-Williams, Christie Manning, Kirra Krygsman, and Meighen Speiser, 2017.
apa.org/news/press/releases/2017/03/mental-health-climate.pdf

"New Approaches to Ecologically Based, Designed Urban Plant Communities in Britain: Do These Have Any Relevance in the United States?" James D. Hitchmough, 2008.
digitalcommons.lmu.edu/cgi/viewcontent.cgi?article=1019&context=cate

"Plant Disease, Plant Pest and Invasive Alien Species Prevention and Control (England) Scheme," Department for Environment, Food and Rural Affairs, 2014.
assets.publishing.service.gov.uk/government/uploads/system/uploads/attachment_data/file/387352/plant-disease-pest-nvasive-alien-species-prevention-control-state-aid.pdf

"Plants in the UK Flower a Month Earlier Under Recent Warming," Ulf Büntgen, Alma Piermattei, Paul J. Krusic, Jan Esper, Tim Sparks, and Alan Crivellaro, 2022.
royalsocietypublishing.org/doi/10.1098/rspb.2021.2456

"RHS Gardening in a Changing Climate," Eleanor Webster, Ross Cameron, and Alistair Culham, 2017.
rhs.org.uk/science/pdf/rhs-gardening-in-a-changing-climate-report.pdf

"Sand, Gravel, and UN Sustainable Development Goals: Conflicts, Synergies, and Pathways Forward," Mette Bendixen, Lars L. Iversen, Jim Best, Daniel M. Franks, Christopher R. Hackney, Edgardo M. Latrubesse, Lucy S. Tusting, 2021.
sciencedirect.com/science/article/abs/pii/S2590332221004097

"Solastalgia: A New Concept in Health and Identity," Glenn Albrecht, 2005.
bridges.monash.edu/articles/journal_contribution/_Solastalgia_a_new_concept_in_health_and_identity/4311905

"The Effects of Marine Sand and Gravel Extraction on the Macrobenthos at a Commercial Dredging Site (results 6 years post-dredging)," S. E. Boyd, D. S. Limpenny, H. L. Rees, K. M. Cooper, 2005.
academic.oup.com/icesjms/article/62/2/145/602082

"Toward Green Concrete for Better Sustainable Environment," Bambang Suhendro, 2014.
sciencedirect.com/science/article/pii/S1877705814032494

"Understanding Climate Change from a Global Analysis of City Analogues," Jean-Francois Bastin, Emily Clark, Thomas Elliott, Simon Hart et al., 2019.
doi.org/10.1371/journal.pone.0217592

WEBSITES

Agroforestry Research Trust, The
Agroforestry is the growing of both trees and agricultural/horticultural crops on the same piece of land—useful advice and resources.
agroforestry.co.uk

British Plastics Federation
Advice and guidance on plastic
bpf.co.uk/Sustainability/Plastics_Recycling.aspx

Charles Dowding—No Dig Gardening
No dig gardening resources and advice
charlesdowding.co.uk

Climate Matching Tool
Match future climates across the globe.
climatematch.org.uk

Current vs. Future Cities
Cities of the future—visualizing climate change to inspire action.
crowtherlab.pageflow.io/cities-of-the-future-visualizing-climate-change-to-inspire-action#213121

Everyday Recycler
General recycling advice
everydayrecycler.com

Forest Monitoring Designed for Action
Global Forest Watch (GFW) is an online platform
that provides data and tools for monitoring forests.
GFW allows anyone to access near real-time
information about how forests are changing.
globalforestwatch.org

Garden Organic
The essence of organic growing is to work within
natural systems and cycles. The basic principle is
that the soil is as important as the plants it supports.
gardenorganic.org.uk/principles

Grey Water Action
Tips and advice on gray water reuse.
greywateraction.org/greywater-choosing-plants-and-
irrigating

Grow Peat-free
Advice on how to grow plants without peat.
growpeatfree.org/whats-in-peat-free

**How to stop invasive non-native plants
from spreading**
Advice and guidance from the UK Government
gov.uk/guidance/prevent-the-spread-of-harmful-invasive-
and-non-native-plants

IPCC
The Intergovernmental Panel on Climate Change
(IPCC) is the United Nations body for assessing the
science related to climate change.
https://www.ipcc.ch/

Mains 2 Rains
Utility water usage in our homes and gardens is often
highest in hot, dry periods when water availability is
lowest. By adopting a few pledges, we can make our
gardens and outdoor spaces thrive on the rainfall we
receive by collecting it and reusing it in dry spells.
mains2rains.uk

Plume Labs
Combating air pollution
plumelabs.com/en

RHS Advice
A huge resource of gardening advice from the RHS
covering a wide range of topics
rhs.org.uk/advice

Biodiversity advice
rhs.org.uk/biodiversity

Disease advice
rhs.org.uk/disease

Gardening for the environment
rhs.org.uk/gardening-for-the-environment

Gardening for wildlife
rhs.org.uk/wildlife

Growing guides for popular plants
rhs.org.uk/plants/popular

Plant problem advice
rhs.org.uk/problems

Sustainability strategy
rhs.org.uk/about-the-rhs/sustainability/sustainability-
strategy-document

Soil Association, The
A charity working with everyone to transform the way
we care for our natural world.
soilassociation.org

Surfers Against Sewage
Clean water action group
sas.org.uk/water-quality

What are SuDS?
A good description of SuDS
ambiental.co.uk/what-are-suds-sustainable-drainage-
systems-guide

HARDINESS ZONES

Zones	Temperature ranges	Category
1	Below −50°F (−46°C)	Severest winter
2	−50° to −40°F (−46° to −40°C)	Severest winter
3	−40° to −30°F (−40° to −34°C)	Severest winter
4	−30° to −20°F (−34° to −29°C)	Severest winter
5	−20° to −10°F (−29° to −23°C)	Cold winter
6	−10° to 0°F (−23° to −18°C)	Cold winter
7	0° to 10°F (−18° to −12°C)	Average winter
8	10° to 20°F (−12° to −7°C)	Mild winter
9	20° to 30°F (−7° to −1°C)	Mild winter
10	30° to 40°F (−1° to 4°C)	Subtropical
11-13	Above 40°F (Above 4°C)	Tropical

02

[01] The first stage was to create a "white card" model. This is an untextured landscape, placing the elements and 3D massing—the shapes and forms. [02] For the next stage, textures were added to the model to bring the design to life, testing elements like reflectiveness of water and the desired level of weathering on the timber.

01

[03] At the final stage, plants were added. Structural plants were placed individually, then underplanting was "scattered" in preselected mixes for a randomized feel. The brief was for the plantings to feel naturalistic and wild.

03

MICHAEL POWELL and **SAM TAYLOR** of AVA CGI created the computer-generated resilient garden in this book from my designs, as well as the existing site before the redesign, and the virtual reality accompaniment. Michael and Sam explain their process here.

"

COMPUTER GENERATED IMAGERY (CGI) HAS COME A LONG WAY; SOME OF THE VISUALS YOU PRODUCED LOOK ALMOST PHOTOREALISTIC. HOW WAS THAT ACHIEVED?

The minimum set-up in the pursuit of photorealism is a combination of detailed 3D modeling, physically based rendering materials (PBR), and image-based lighting. Images and animations can then be exported using a path tracing renderer, which is currently the most accurate way of representing global illumination (the way light bounces off and through objects). However, most professionals within the CG industry would agree that photorealism lies within surface imperfections, be they cracks in paint, dust on a vase, or fingerprints on a pane of glass—imperfections are everywhere in the real world, and these subtleties can trick the eye into believing that a 3D image is real.

HOW DO YOU SOURCE THE PLANTS? SOME OF THE 3D MODELS ARE STUNNING IN THEIR DETAIL.

Modeling organic assets such as plants can be complex and time-consuming, often requiring specialist software to achieve good results. Over the years, we have built up a library of professional-grade 3D plant models by either creating them ourselves or purchasing from online stores. Studying and recording flora is essential for accurate modeling and texturing; a simple leaf has many properties that require capturing for realism. This information is then fed into a PBR material in the form of dedicated images that dictate such details as color, transparency, and reflectancy.

LIGHTING AND FRAMING ARE KEY TO SHOWING THE MODEL SUCCESSFULLY. HAVE YOU ANY TIPS ON HOW TO GET THE SHOTS RIGHT?

There are many rules of thumb about what creates a pleasing image; ultimately, we aim to lead the viewer toward a subject to explore further. The eye will always focus on the brightest part of an image first, so it is good practice to position the focal point in the most exposed area of the scene. A dappled lighting effect is also used in many of the images where light filters through the trees, creating atmosphere and interest.

Additionally, using compositional guides is an effective way to structure and balance an image. If you look closely, you may identify where principles such as symmetry, the golden ratio, and the rule of thirds have been used within the book's CGIs.

ACKNOWLEDGMENTS

PICTURE CREDITS

The publisher would like to thank the following for their kind permission to reproduce their photographs:

(Key: a-above; b-below/bottom; c-center; f-far; l-left; r-right; t-top)

Page 8: t **Tom Massey**, b **Britt Willoughby Dyer**; **10: Alamy Stock Photo**/Marek Stepan; **11:** b **Shutterstock**/FLPA; **12:** t **Alamy Stock Photo**/Will Perrett, b **Chris Leather** www.cornawlls.co.uk; **15:** t **Alamy Stock Photo**/P Tomlins, bl **Samuel North**, br **Tom Massey**; **16:** t **Dirk-Jan Visser**, b **Britt Willoughby Dyer**; **17:** t **Britt Willoughby Dyer**, b **Dirk-Jan Visser**, **19:** t **Britt Willoughby Dyer**, b **Alamy Stock Photo**/PA Images; **20-21: Noshe**; **24: Dreamstime**/SJors737; **25:** t **Getty Images**/Saeed Khan/AFP, b **Dreamstime**/Silkenphotography; **27: Alamy Stock Photo**/Mauritius images GmbH; **29:** t and b **Alister Thorpe**; **30-31: Alamy Stock Photo**/Duncan Cuthbertson; **32 and 33: Harvey Wang**; **35:** t **GAP Photos**/Stephen Studd-Sam Ovens, b **Britt Willoughby Dyer**; **36 Francis Augusto**; **44: Britt Willoughby Dyer**; **46: Ed Reeve**; **48-49: Nigel Dunnett**; **49:** b **Britt Willoughby Dyer**; **50:** t **Britt Willoughby Dyer**, b **Alister Thorpe**; **50-51:** b **Alister Thorpe**; **51:** br **Shutterstock**/Alison Hancock; **52:** tl **Alamy Stock Photo**/Pat Tuson, tr **Dreamstime**/Niradj, bl **Alamy Stock Photo**/Jeffrey Blackley, br **Richard Bloom**; **53: Nigel Dunnett**; **55:** t **Dreamstime**/Stevendalewhite, b **Shutterstock**/RHJ Photos; **56: GAP Photos**/Annette Lepple; **57:** tl **GAP Photos**/Maddie Thornhill, tr **GAP Photos**/Ernie Janes, c **Marianne Majerus**/RHS Garden Wisley, Designer: James Hitchmough, bl **Britt Willoughby Dyer**, br **Tim Green**; **58: Alamy Stock Photo**/RM Flavio Massari; **62: GAP Photos**/Jonathan Buckley – Demonstrated by Nick Bailey; **63:** t **Alister Thorpe**, b **Marianne Majerus**/Designer: Thomas Doxiadis; **69:** tl **Dreamstime**/Andrii Kozlytskyi, tr **Dreamstime**/Marek Uliasz, cl **Dreamstime**/Atthaphol Sileung, cr **Shutterstock**/Govindamadhava 108, b **Dreamstime**/ Larisa Rudenko; **72:** t **Alamy Stock Photo**/Appeal Photos, b **Alamy Stock Photo**/Larry Geddis; **75:** t **Sarah Price**/design: Sarah Price and Nigel Dunnett, b **Alamy Stock Photo**/eye35; **76:** t **Nigel Dunnett**, b **GAP Photos**/Michael King; **82: Alamy Stock Photo**/Rudmer Zwerver; **83:** b **Jay Davey Bespoke Willow**; **86: Clive Nichols**; **88: Dreamstime**/Bojana Zuzu; **89: Britt Willoughby Dyer**; **90:** t **Shutterstock**/Amelia Armstrong, b **Britt Willoughby Dyer**; **112: Sarah Cuttle**; **124:** tl and tr **Dreamstime**/Graham Corney, b **Dreamstime**/Shamils, 120: **Rob Cardillo**; **125:** t **Dreamstime**/Darren Curzone, bc **Dreamstime**/Shawn Hempel, b **Dreamstime**/Marilyn Barbone; **130 Britt Willoughby Dyer**; **164:** tl **GAP Photos**/Nova Photo Graphik, tc **GAP Photos**/Tommy Tonsberg, tr **GAP Photos**/Jason Ingram, b **GAP Photos**/Fiona Rice; **165:** l **GAP Photos**/Maddie Thornhill, r **Dorling Kindersley**/Mark Winwood/Hampton Court Flower Show 2014; **166:** l **Dreamstime**/Whiskybottle, r **GAP Photos**/Elke Borkowski, **167:** t **Marianne Majerus**, bl **Dorling Kindersley**/Mark Winwood/RHS Wisley, br **GAP Photos**/Jason Ingram; **168:** tl **Dreamstime**/Iva Vagnerova, tr **Dreamstime**/Orest Lyzhechka, bl **GAP Photos**/Robert Mabic, br **GAP Photos**/Tim Gainey; **169:** tl **Dorling Kindersley**/Andrew Lawson, tc **Dorling Kindersley**/Mark Winwood/RHS Wisley, tr **Dorling Kindersley**/Neil

Fletcher, b **Dreamstime**/Tikhonova Vera; **172:** tl **Dreamstime**/Apugach 5, tc **GAP Photos**/Sarah Cuttle, tr **GAP Photos**/Howard Rice, b **GAP Photos**/Charles Hawes; **173:** tl **Marianne Majerus**, tr and b **GAP Photos**/Torrie Chugg, **174: Shutterstock**/Vladislav Marvin, **178:** l **GAP Photos**/Andrea Jones, c **GAP Photos**/Richard Bloom, r **GAP Photos**/Howard Rice; **179:** l **Marianne Majerus**, c **GAP Photos** Dianna Jazwinski, r **GAP Photos**/Ernie Janes; **188:** l **Dorling Kindersley**/Peter Anderson, c **GAP Photos**/Nova Photo Graphik, **188-189: GAP Photos** Evgeniya Vlasova; **189** r **GAP Photos**/Nova Photo Graphik; **190:** t **Dorling Kindersley**/Mark Winwood/RHS Wisley, c **GAP Photos**/Heather Edwards, r **GAP Photos** Gary Smith; **191:** l **GAP Photos**/Gary Smith, r **GAP Photos**/Richard Bloom; **192:** tl **GAP Photos**/Fiona Lea, tc **GAP Photos**/Fiona McLeod, tr and b **GAP Photos**/Jonathan Buckley; **193:** tl **GAP Photos**/John Glover, tc **GAP Photos**/Mark Bolton, tr **Alamy Stock Photo**/Blickwinkel, b **GAP Photos**/Mark Turner; **194:** l **Dorling Kindersley**/Mark Winwood/RHS Wisley, r **GAP Photos**/Jonathan Buckley; **195:** l **GAP Photos**/Julie Dansereau – Loseley Park, r **GAP Photos**/Jason Ingram, **196:** tl **GAP Photos**/Jo Whitworth, bl **Dorling Kindersley**/Brian North, r **GAP Photos**/Juliette Wade; **197:** t **GAP Photos**/Jonathan Buckley, b **Dreamstime**/Igor Dolgov; **198: Tom Massey**; **202:** l **Dorling Kindersley**/RHS Tatton Park, **202-203: Dreamstime**/Milanvachan, **203:** r **GAP Photos**/Nova Photo Graphik, **204:** l **GAP Photos**/Geoff Kidd, c **GAP Photos**/Ernie Janes, **204-205: GAP Photos**/Bjorn Hansson, **205:** r **GAP Photos**/John Glover, **208: Shutterstock**/haveseen, **213:** t **Shutterstock**/Amit kg, b **Dreamstime**/Seadam, **214:** t **Dreamstime**/Wuttichok, c **Shutterstock**/Wong Gunkid, b **Dreamstime**/Bert Folsom, **215:** t **Dreamstime**/Harald Biebel, c **Dreamstime**/Krishna Maharana111, b **Dreamstime**/Gualtiero Boffi, **216-217:** b **Alamy Stock Photo**/Jaramír Chalabala, **217:** t **Dreamstime**/Andreadonetti, **218:** t and b **cedstone.co.uk, 219:** l and c **London Stone**, r **Alamy Stock Photo**/Panther Media GmbH, **220:** t **GAP Photos**/Andrea Jones – Design Beth Chatto, b **GAP Photos**/Mark Bolton – Prospect Cottage, Derek Jarman; **222: Arcaid**; **225:** tl **GAP Photos**/Rob Whitworth – Designer Sarah Price, bl **Alamy Stock Photo**/Selecta, r **Rublazzo; 226: Shutterstock**/Aldarhino; **229: Deborah Husk; 230:** t **Alister Thorpe**, b **Britt Willoughby Dyer; 231: Britt Willoughby Dyer; 232 and 233: Dreamstime** and **Shutterstock; 235:** t **Shutterstock**/ Taechit Tanantornanutra, bl **Dreamstime**/Candy 1812, br **Alamy Stock Photo**/Kevin Foy; **236:** t **Alamy Stock Photo**/Kevin Walker, cl **Alamy Stock Photo**/Dave Bevan, bl **Dreamstime**/Joel Gafford, br **Dreamstime**/Europixel; **237:** tl **Dreamstime**/Marek Uliasz, tr **Alamy Stock Photo**/RM Floral, c **Shutterstock** Worawit Sanasri, bl **Shutterstock**/Kolidzei, br **Alamy Stock Photo**/Alexandra Scotcher; **239:** tl **The Living**, Photo: Amy Barkow, tr **Stone Cycling**/Dim Baslem, br **Marianne Majerus**; **256 Wax London**.

Images on the following pages © **AVA CGI**: 2, 80, 95, 97, 98–99, 100–110, 115, 116, 123, 127, 128, 132, 137, 138, 141, 142–143, 145, 147, 149, 150–151, 152, 154, 158–159, 161, 162–163, 170–171, 176–177, 181, 182, 185, 186–187, 201, 248.

FROM TOM

Writing my first book has been a journey of discovery, forcing me to reflect and review my own practice and priorities. Having time to research, reflect, and share my findings though words, designs, and ideas has been a privilege—one that I have many people to thank for.

Firstly, my wife Anna, for unswerving support. My life has often been consumed by my profession and she has been patient and supportive even when my time for friends and family has been limited. Anna's eye for detail and gift for writing makes her the perfect sounding board.

Thanks to the DK team, whose knowledge, skill, and support made writing this book hugely rewarding. Chris, Ruth, Max, and Katie, for their belief, trust, and a shared vision. Sophie, Barbara, and Diana for keeping everything on track and pushing with creative design and editorial comments.

Thanks to the designers: Alex with initial concepts and Vicky with layouts and book design, keeping it collaborative and graphically exciting. Thanks to AVA CGI, Michael and Sam, for bringing the garden concepts to life in stunning detail. Deserving of a special mention are photographers Britt and Alister, who have captured my work so beautifully, and picture researcher Emily for all of her hard work finding and sourcing images to illustrate the text.

Thank you to the interviewees: Je, John, Martin, Olivier, Sarah, Tayshan, Tijana, and Thomas, for taking time to share your knowledge, expertise, and experience.

A big thank you to the RHS for trusting me to write this book. Access to the RHS science team has been invaluable, and a special mention goes to Tijana, who has been supportive and critical, linking to other members of the science team, ensuring the book is grounded in real RHS research and is true to the RHS aims: to enrich people's lives through plants and to make the world a greener and more beautiful place.

Finally, thank you to my mother, for connecting me with nature from a young age. I hope this book inspires others to garden and grow.

FROM THE PUBLISHER

The publisher would like to thank Tom Morse for his help with technical prepress, Michael Powell and Sam Taylor of AVA CGI, Jane Simmonds for the proofread, and Ruth Ellis for the index.

Senior Editor Sophie Blackman
Senior US Editor Kayla Dugger
Senior Designer Barbara Zuniga
Production Editor David Almond
Production Controller Rebecca Parton
Jackets and Sales Material Coordinator
Jasmin Lennie
DTP and Design Coordinator Heather Blagden
Editorial Manager Ruth O'Rourke
Design Manager Marianne Markham
Art Director Maxine Pedliham
Publishing Director Katie Cowan

Editor Diana Vowles
Designer Vicky Read
Picture Researcher Emily Hedges
Consultant Gardening Publisher Chris Young
Design Styling Concept Alex Hunting Studio
Illustrator Andrew Torrens
VR AVA CGI

ROYAL HORTICULTURAL SOCIETY
Consultant Simon Maughan
Publisher Helen Griffin

First American Edition, 2023
Published in the United States by DK Publishing
1745 Broadway, 20th Floor, New York, NY 10019

Copyright © 2023 Dorling Kindersley Limited
DK, a Division of Penguin Random House LLC
23 24 25 26 27 10 9 8 7 6 5 4 3 2 1
001–332466–Apr/2023

For the curious
www.dk.com

MIX
Paper | Supporting
responsible forestry
FSC™ C018179

This book was made with Forest Stewardship Council™ certified paper - one small step in DK's commitment to a sustainable future. **For more information go to** www.dk.com/our-green-pledge

Tom Massey is an award-winning garden designer and principal designer at Tom Massey Studio. He strives to produce sustainable gardens that support wildlife, promote biodiversity, and support the local environment.

After growing up in southwest London, Tom graduated from the London College of Garden Design at the Royal Botanic Gardens, Kew, where he is now a visiting tutor. He founded Tom Massey Studio in 2015 and designs gardens for private and commercial clients, public spaces, shows, and festivals in the UK and overseas.

Tom has designed and exhibited two gardens at the RHS Chelsea Flower Show: in 2018, he was awarded an RHS Silver-Gilt Medal for the Lemon Tree Trust Garden, and in 2021, the Yeo Valley Organic Garden received an RHS Gold Medal and the BBC People's Choice Award.

In 2020, he designed the planting scheme for the "Hothouse" installation: a collaboration with Studio Weave for the London Design Festival. In 2022, he received an award from the Society of Garden Designers for an outstanding residential garden in Twickenham, London.

Tom featured on the BBC television series *Your Garden Made Perfect*, designing gardens focused on supporting wildlife, promoting biodiversity, and experimenting with growing mediums. *Resilient Garden* is his first book.